ANIMAL
ENCYCLOPEDIA

igloo

igloo

This edition published in 2007
by Igloo Books Ltd
Cottage Farm,
Sywell,
NN6 0BJ

www.igloo-books.com

Copyright © 2007 Igloo Books Ltd

All rights reserved. No part of this publication may be reproduced,
stored in a retrieval system, or transmitted in any way or by any means, electronic,
mechanical, photocopying, recording or otherwise, without the prior written
permission of the publisher.

Cataloguing in Publication Data information
10 9 8 7 6 5 4 3 2 1

ISBN: 978-1-84561-685-4

Produced by Metro Media Ltd
Authors: Nathan Hamilton, Deborah Chancellor
Design & layout: Carol Davis
With thanks to: Belinda Weber

Cover image: Munday Hackett/Photographer's Direct
Photography: Ardea, Natural Visions, istock.com, shutterstock.com, photos.com

Printed in China

ICONS EXPLAINED:
- LAND
- SEA/WATER
- AIR

Contents

- 8 Classification
- 10 Classification

12 Invertebrates

- 14 Sponges and simple animals
- 16 Jellyfish, corals and sea anemones
- 18 Worms
- 20 Slugs and snails
- 22 Limpets and whelks
- 24 Conches, cowries and cone shells
- 26 Bivalves
- 28 Squid and octopuses
- 30 Krill, shrimp and lobsters
- 32 Crabs
- 34 Centipedes and millipedes
- 36 Springtails, silverfish, thrips and lice
- 38 Dragonflies
- 40 Termites and earwigs
- 42 Crickets and grasshoppers
- 44 Cockroaches and mantids
- 46 Stick and leaf insects
- 48 True bugs
- 50 Lacewings and caddis flies
- 52 Flies
- 54 Butterflies and moths
- 56 Bees and wasps
- 58 Ants
- 60 Ladybugs, stags and titans
- 62 Fireflies and bombardiers
- 64 Sea stars and sea urchins
- 66 Spiders
- 68 Scorpions
- 70 Sea spiders and horseshoe crabs

72 Fish

74 Jawless fish
76 Rays and skates
78 Sharks
80 Coelacanths, lungfish and arapaima
82 Shoaling fish
84 Migratory fish
86 Deep water fish
88 Bottom feeders
90 Coral reef fish
92 Freshwater fish
94 Eels and catfish
96 Flying fish, seahorses, pipefish and sea dragons
98 Hunting fish

100 Amphibians

102 Newts and salamanders
104 Frogs
106 Toads

108 Reptiles

- 110 Tortoises and turtles
- 112 Pythons and boas
- 114 Venomous snakes
- 116 Devils, monsters and chameleons
- 118 Iguana, geckos and skinks
- 120 Slow worms, skinks and tuataras
- 122 Alligators and crocodiles

124 Birds

- 126 Flightless birds
- 128 Game birds
- 130 Waterfowl
- 132 Shore birds
- 134 Birds of prey
- 136 Parrots
- 138 Nocturnal birds
- 140 Swifts and hummingbirds
- 142 Toucans and hornbills
- 144 Perching birds
- 146 Song birds
- 148 Weavers and creepers
- 150 Courtship displays

5

152 Mammals

- 154 Echidna and platypus
- 156 Bandicoots, wombats and quolls
- 158 Kangaroos and koalas
- 160 Sloths, anteaters and armadillos
- 162 Shrews, moles and hedgehogs
- 164 Bats and flying mammals
- 166 Rabbits and hares
- 168 Small rodents
- 170 Big rodents
- 172 Elephants and hyraxes
- 174 Horses
- 176 Rhinos and tapirs
- 178 Pigs and peccaries
- 180 Cattle
- 182 Goats and sheep
- 184 Deer and antelopes
- 186 Pronghorns and giraffes
- 188 Civets and mongooses
- 190 Small cats
- 192 Lions, leopards and cheetahs
- 194 Tigers, jaguars and pumas
- 196 Bears
- 198 Sun and ice bears
- 200 Raccoons and pandas
- 202 Dogs and foxes
- 204 Hyenas and aardwolves
- 206 Weasels, badgers and skunks
- 208 Otters
- 210 Baleen whales
- 212 Toothed whales
- 214 Dolphins and porpoises
- 216 Seals, sealions and walruses
- 218 Manatees and dugongs
- 220 Camels, alpacas and llamas
- 222 Monkeys and baboons
- 224 Lesser primates
- 226 New World monkeys
- 228 Apes
- 230 Endangered animals
- 232 Conservation
- 234 Index

How living organisms are classified

On the basis of sharing certain similar characteristics, biologists divide living organisms into different groups. They do this through examining DNA and studying a living organism's physical characteristics and how they relate to any other. This is to help them understand the world and how all forms of life have evolved to work within it. You could say scientists have organized a large filing system with which forms of life can be checked and then ordered and classified in groups. As the groups get smaller, the animals are more closely related.

The largest files or groups are called Kingdoms and there are five of them:

1) bacteria, which are single-celled life forms;
2) protists, which are also single-celled, but are larger and more complex;
3) fungi, which live on dead things or their remains;
4) plants, which live by absorbing energy from the sun through photosynthesis; and
5) animals, which are made of many cells and can move around and eat food.

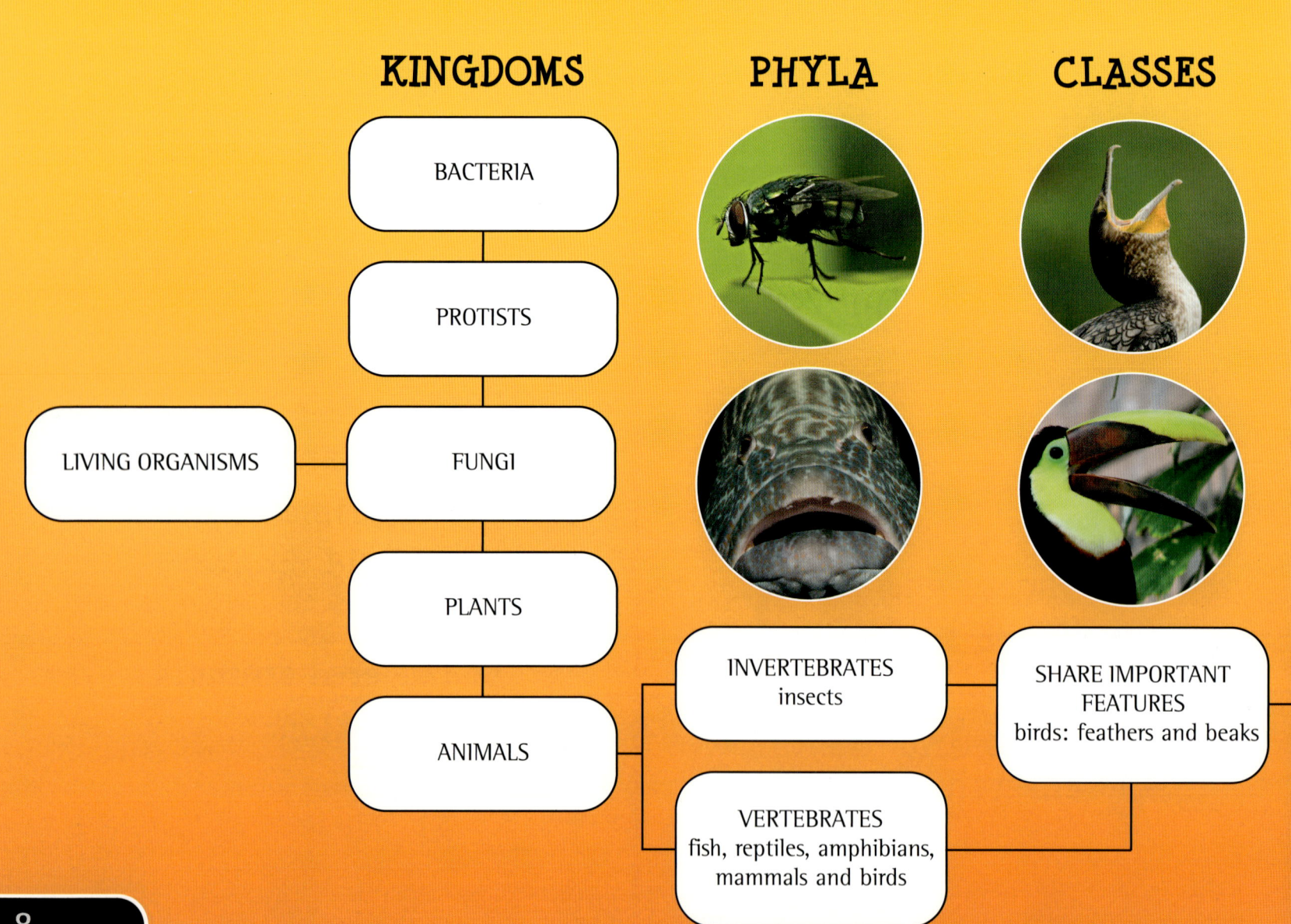

Like all kingdoms, the Animal Kingdom then divides up into different Phyla. Phyla are groups of animals that have evolved from a common ancestor and share similar physical (and physiological) characteristics. For example, fish, reptiles and birds are all in the same Phylum because they all have a backbone.

Phyla are divided into Classes, which are made up of animals that share important features. Birds are all part of the same class of animals, for example, because they all have feathers and beaks.

Classes divide into orders, within which the animals are more closely related and share certain similar distinguishing characteristics: frogs and toads, for example, are part of the same order.

Orders divide up into Families, all members sharing a common feature that distinguishes them from other orders: the giant fruit bat and the common pipistrelle bat are part of the same family because they both have a forearm adapted as a wing.

Families then divide up into Genera, in which animals tend to be very closely related: a dingo and a wolf are part of the same Genus. And Genera are divided into the many different individual Species in our world.

So far, biologists have classified around two million different animals, and some estimate there could be as many as 30 million to find. It may be the case that we will never know all of the amazing animal species that live on our planet.

ORDERS — SIMILAR CHARACTERISTICS — frogs and toads

FAMILIES — SHARING A COMMON FEATURE — giant fruit bat and pipistrelle bat: forearm adapted as a wing

GENERA — VERY CLOSELY RELATED — dingo and wolf

SPECIES — TWO MILLION ANIMALS ARE CLASSIFIED

The Animal Kingdom

PHYLA:

Simple Animals
Simple animals have no heads or special sense organs like eyes. They include sponges and rotifers.

Roundworms
Roundworms have long, cylindrical bodies with no legs and are covered by a skin, and they often live in the soil or inside living things.

Flatworms
Flatworms have paper-thin, legless bodies. Most flatworms live in water or inside other animals. They move by sliding or swimming.

Nemertean Worms
Mostly marine but there are a few that live on land.

Segmented Worms
As their name suggests, segmented worms' bodies are divided into rings or segments. Many species, including earthworms, live in soil, while others live in water.

Cnidarians
Cnidarians are bell-like or bag-shaped animals with tentacles. Most cnidarians live in the sea and include jellyfish, corals and sea anemones.

Echinoderms
Echinoderms, like starfish and sea urchins, have bodies that are divided into five identical parts. They all live in water.

Mollusks
Mollusks, like snails or slugs, have soft bodies that aren't divided into segments. Many mollusks have a shell, but others, like the octopus or squid, do not.

Arthropods
Arthropods' bodies are covered in a hard casing, called an exoskeleton. Arthropods have several pairs of jointed legs. Arthropods include: crustaceans, which have two pairs of antennae or feelers; chelicerates, which have do not have any antennae and feed through special mouthparts called chelicerae; and uniramians, which only one pair of antennae, and multiple pairs of legs.

Chordates
Chordates have an internal skeleton and a strong, supporting rod down their backs. In more highly developed chordates, such as reptiles, birds and mammals, this rod is well developed and is called a backbone. In less well-developed chordates, such as sea squirts, the rod is much simpler in structure and is called a notochord.

10

CLASSES:

Jawless Fish

Jawless fish have long, thin bodies, with large sucker-like mouths.

Cartilaginous Fish

Some fish, the cartilaginous fish, have skeletons made of cartilage, not bone. Sharks and rays are cartilaginous fish, and have stiff fins.

Bony Fish

The skeletons of bony fish, as their name suggests, are made of bone, and their skin is covered with small, overlapping scales.

Amphibians

Amphibians live partly in water and partly on land, and all change their shape completely as they grow. For example, frogs start out life as tadpoles, then grow limbs and lose their tails. The little froglets climb out of the water and live on land as adults, returning to the water to mate.

Reptiles

Reptiles are cold-blooded animals with scaly skin. Most reptiles lay eggs, but some species of snake give birth to live young.

Birds

All birds have wings, beaks and feathers, but not all can fly. Birds are warm-blooded animals that lay eggs.

Mammals

Mammals are warm-blooded animals with bodies covered in fur or hair that suckle their young (feed them milk). Most mammals give birth to live young, but three very primitive species, called monotremes, lay eggs.

Invertebrates

Invertebrates are animals that don't have backbones. They make up the majority of animal life on the planet, with estimates reaching 95-97 percent of all species. They range from some of the smallest animals on land, like springtails, to some of the largest in the oceans, like the giant squid, and they exist in every habitat on Earth.

Because there are so many of them, the organization of invertebrates is quite complicated. Arthropods (which have a hard outer covering, called an exoskeleton) make up the largest group ('phylum'), containing a huge number of different types of animals. These include lobsters and crabs, spiders, scorpions, horseshoe crabs, and the biggest batch – insects.

Insects (or Insecta) are in fact the largest class of all animals, with more named species than any other. There are over one million of them named so far – more than all the other groups of known animals combined!

Sponges and simple animals

An animal is a living thing that has many cells and eats food. Simple animals do not have heads or special sensory organs like eyes. The simplest animals are often not visible to the naked eye but some are much larger, like sponges. Single-celled life forms are called 'protozoans' and almost all live in water, as well as most simple animals. This is why some scientists believe life started in the oceans – most examples of the likely earliest forms have been found there.

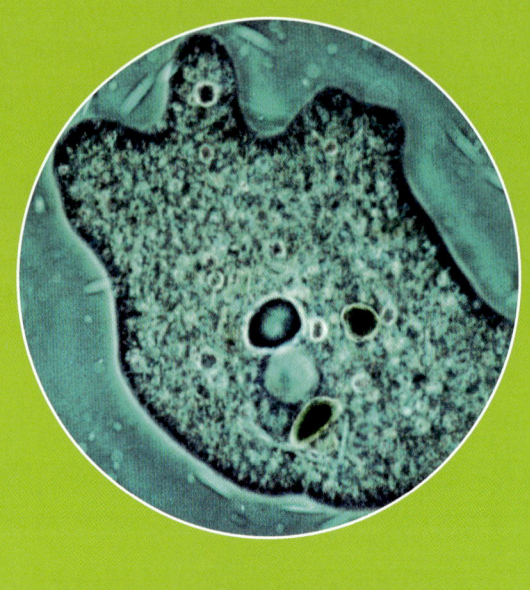

 *Protozoans like amebas date back over 1 billion years – that's 10,000 years older than humans.*

▲ What do amebas look like?

Amebas are microscopic and cannot be seen with the naked eye because they are made of only one cell. Under a microscope, many look like blobs of jelly. They have no set shape, but some build themselves a type of shell casing, although most have no hard parts at all. They move by pushing in the direction they want to go, which slowly takes the rest of the cell with it. Amebas feed by following smaller life forms, then surrounding and absorbing them.

 *Water bears can hibernate in a drought-resistant state for up to 25 years.*

◀ What are water bears?

Water bears are found in puddles and freshwater pools – they move around slowly on eight short, stubby legs. They have elongated barrel-shaped bodies and feed off the juices of other animals and plants like moss. Water bears are also called tardigrades and, like all life, they need water to stay alive. In the absence of water, however, they are strong survivors and can hibernate until conditions improve. When they are in their hibernating state, they are called a 'tun'.

What is a breadcrumb sponge?

Sponges are widespread throughout temperate and tropical seas. They usually have a thread-like skeleton made of keratin – the same material as hair and nails. The breadcrumb sponge forms flat over rocks where it feeds by sucking in water through small round pores dotted all over its surface, filtering it for food. It is called a breadcrumb sponge because it is quite fragile and crumbles like breadcrumbs if it is touched.

The breadcrumb sponge is found in the Mediterranean Sea and the Atlantic and Pacific Oceans.

How many species of sponge are there? Over 5,000 have been found so far.

▶ Why do sea oranges smell?

The sulfur sponge – or sea orange – can be found living on rocks or even on the shells of some hermit crabs. It forms smooth, rounded, flattened or spherical growths of fleshy tissue and is an orangey-yellow color. It is called a sulfur sponge because of its sulfurous smell – caused by the sulfur in its toxic mucus, which it produces as a defense against predators. However, it doesn't upset the hermit crabs that sometimes carry it around on their shells as camouflage from octopus predators.

Sometimes sea oranges dissolve the whole of a hermit crab's shell, and so provide it with all of its protection.

15

Jellyfish, corals and sea anemones

Jellyfish, corals and sea anemones belong to a group of animals know as cnidarians. This name means 'stingers' because many cnidarians can sting, either as a defense or to catch food. They do this with complex capsules called nematocysts. Cnidarians have mouths encircled by tentacles and hollow box- or bell-shaped bodies. Some corals group together and form reefs. Reefs are important places to live for many other forms of life. Jellyfish are some of the most poisonous animals on Earth, and anemones are some of the most familiar and attractive forms of life in the oceans.

How do jellyfish swim?

The saucer jelly swims by relaxing and contracting the edge of its bell-shaped top. This moves it along by pushing water away behind it. Beneath the bell is a square mouth with four mouth-arms hanging down from the corners. Jellyfish eat by stinging fish with their tentacles around the rim of its bells and then drawing them towards their mouths with these mouth-arms. Their bells have a network of thin canals that extends from the middle and distributes food and digestive juices around the rest of the body.

▼ Are jellyfish dangerous to humans?

Flecker's box jellyfish (also known as the Australian box jellyfish) is the largest and most dangerous box jelly. Their powerful stinging tentacles hang down in groups of 16 attached to four 'pedaliums' at the bottom of the bell and can grow up to 6 feet 6 inches/ 2 meters long. When the box jellyfish's tentacles brush against another animal, they explode into microscopic, thread-like fibers, each ending in a hypodermic barb that injects powerful venom.

Saucer jellyfish grow to between 5 and 6 inches/12 and 15 centimeters in diameter.

The box jellyfish has been responsible for hundreds of deaths and is so powerful it can kill a person in three minutes.

16

▶ What is coral made of?

Corals, such as staghorn coral, are actually supporting skeletons holding colonies of animals called polyps. Coral polyps form colonies by making buds that grow into new polyps. The way they do this determines the shape of the coral. Some types of coral polyp grow a hard casing made out of a chalky substance as a protection, and these casings can stick together to form huge reefs. Polyps feed at night by stinging and catching small animals in their tentacles.

 *The Great Barrier Reef in Australia is the largest structure ever built by any living thing.*

How old are the cnidarians? Fossils have been found that are over 500 million years old.

▼ Where do sea anemones live?

Like most species of sea anemones, the dahlia anemone has a sac-like body with finger-like tentacles, and a foot that fastens it to rocks. Some anemones also live in sand. Anemones feed like other cnidarians, by stinging their prey and moving it towards their mouths to digest using their simple stomachs and digestive system. An anemone is a cnidarian that develops from a polyp without a medusa, or jellyfish, stage. Instead they can reproduce by budding, ejecting eggs and sperm into the water, or even splitting in two.

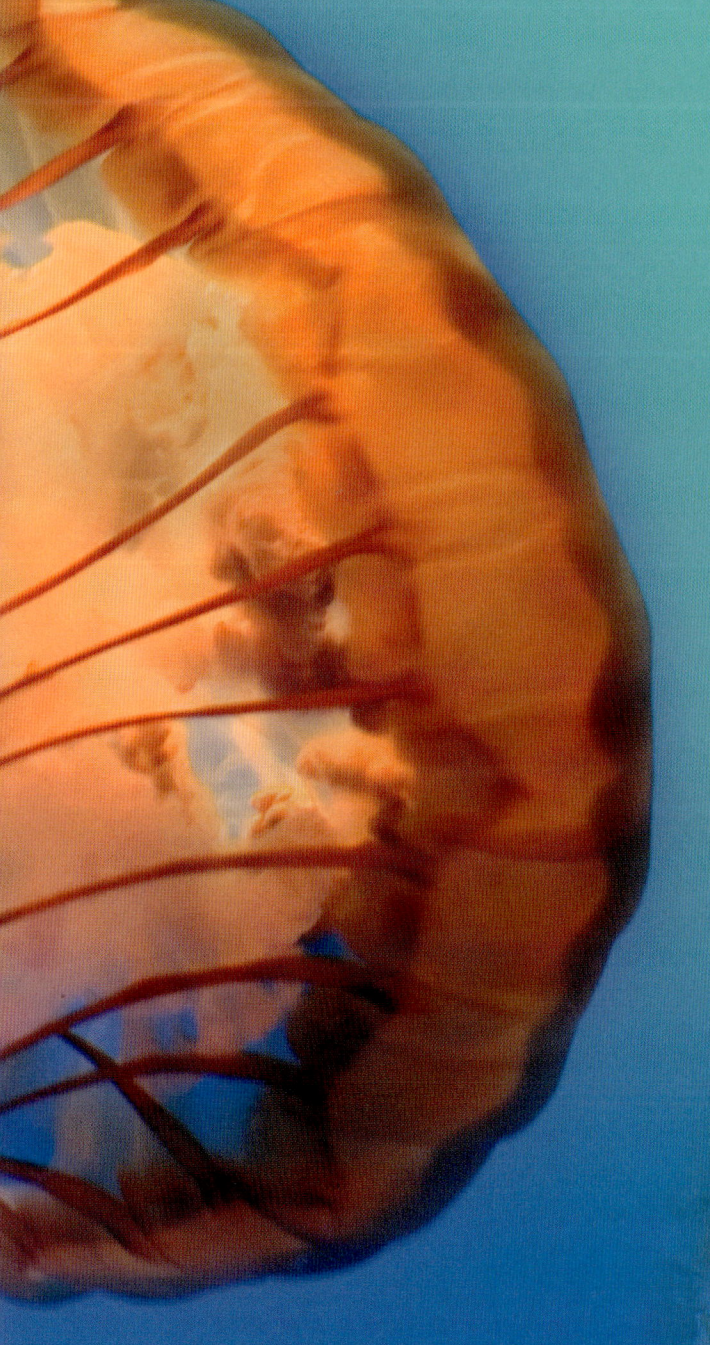

 *Sea anemones are so named because of their resemblance to flowers of the same name.*

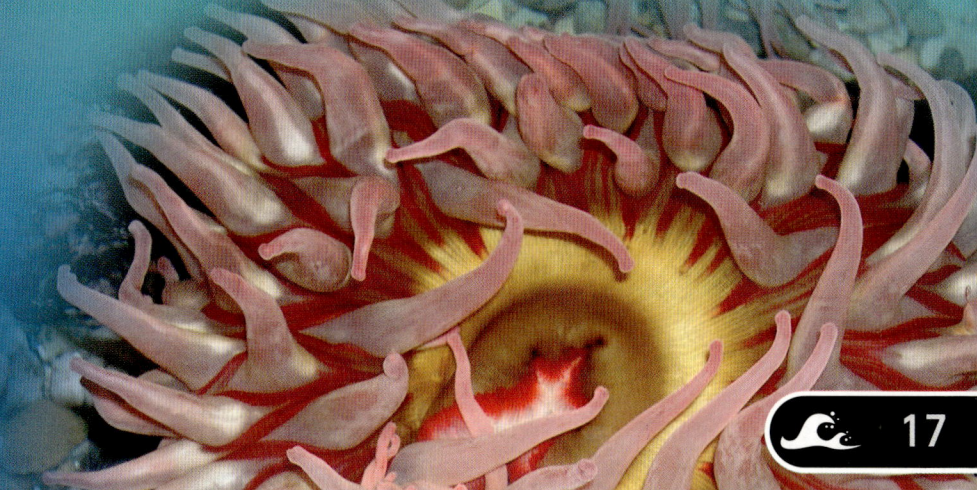

Worms

Any soft-bodied, legless animal with a length that exceeds its width is probably a worm. There are many different types. Most well-known are the earthworms, which are segmented worms, so called because their bodies are made up of different compartments, or segments. Other types of worm include parasites, such as nematodes, tapeworms and flukes, leeches and flatworms. Worms are found everywhere, even in the most inhospitable places on the planet.

Where do you find Pompeii worms?

Pompeii worms are found very deep down in the Pacific Ocean in temperatures that are nearly hot enough to boil water. They cluster on the side of hydrothermal vent chimneys, close to where hot water and gases emerge from inside the Earth and spew into the sea. The temperatures here average 149°F/65°C, so Pompeii worms are the most heat-tolerant animals on Earth. These worms grow to about 4 inches/10 centimeters in length.

▼ What is a flatworm?

Flatworms are the simplest type of worm and they have flat bodies that can be very thin. Many are parasites, like the dog tapeworm. This creature has a round head that attaches to the inside of a dog's intestines with sharp hooks. From here, it feeds on the partially digested food that passes through the gut from the dog's stomach. Sections of the worm drop off at its rear, carrying eggs outside the body. These eggs can infect another dog.

When were Pompeii worms discovered? Only as recently as 1986!

Cat tapeworms have flat, ribbon-like bodies with up to 150 segments.

18

How do you tell male and female earthworms apart?

Both male and female organs are present in each individual, so you can't! Common earthworms are a type of segmented worm that are found all across the world. They do a vital job of breaking down waste materials and improving the soil. An earthworm's body is divided into about 150 ring-like segments and it breathes through its skin. They live in moist, rich soil at depths of about 1 foot/30 centimeters. In the winter, earthworms dig deeper, away from frost, and lie coiled up in soil chambers.

Earthworms can consume up to one-third of their own body weight in just one day.

▶ Where do vent worms live?

Vent worms live deep under the Pacific Ocean, near where cracks in the Earth's surface cause temperatures to rise. Chemicals and molten substances from deep in the Earth's center form huge chimney-like structures, around which vent worms live. Vent worms feed with the help of billions of bacteria inside their red gills that convert harmful sulphurous chemicals collected from the vents into energy. These remarkable creatures can survive in sea temperatures of up to 131°F/55°C. They live in long white tubes, which may grow to about 10 feet/3 meters long.

The vent worm, Riftia pachyptila, lives at depths of over 1 mile/1.6 kilometers in the Pacific Ocean.

19

Slugs and snails

Slugs and snails are a type of mollusk known as gastropods (which means 'stomach foot') after their single, slimy suction-pad of a foot-muscle which they use to creep along. There are about 75,000 species of gastropods now known on land and in the sea, which makes them the largest class of mollusks. Slugs and snails eat plants and are considered pests as they devour crops and flowers. Their mouths are lined with rows of tiny teeth, that wear down one after the other.

▼ **What is the largest land snail?**

The biggest land-dwelling snail in the world is the giant African snail. It can weigh more than 1lbs 12oz/800kg, which is nearly as much as a bag of sugar. Its body can reach 1 foot/30 centimeters long and its shell alone can be as large as 8 inches/20 centimeters long – bigger than a soccer ball! It has been introduced from Africa into other warm countries as a pet, in zoos, or as a source of food. In many of these countries, it is now a pest as it has no natural predators.

Gastropods like the garden snail have one-part shell, so they are called 'univalves'.

For farmers, the giant land snail is southeast Asia's most destructive pest.

◀ **How does the garden snail survive in dry weather?**

The garden snail survives dry spells by finding as dark and damp a place as it can and then retreating far into its shell to preserve moisture. It leaves a layer of mucus around the edges of the outside that dries and sticks tight to the surface it is on. It also seals off the outside with dried mucus, leaving a 'door'. A snail's shell provides plenty of protection. Its vital organs are housed within it and the shell grows in a spiral as the snail grows. Like all mollusk shells, a snail's shell is made from a tough substance called calcium carbonate.

▶ Why do slugs and snails leave a trail of slime?

Like all slugs and snails, the great black slug needs moisture to survive. It travels along the ground over a layer of slimy mucus. It is this mucus that causes its trail. To produce this mucus, its body needs to have a higher than average water content. The great black slug eats rotting vegetation and even the dead bodies of other slugs. It has a breathing hole behind its head on the right-hand side and, like other slugs and snails, it uses tentacles that can touch and smell to find food.

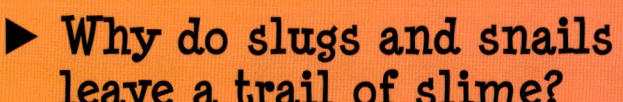

Like other gastropods, slugs lay eggs. When they hatch, baby slugs look like miniature adults.

How fast is a garden snail? It is quite fast: 0.5 inches/1.3 centimeters a second top speed (that's fast, for a snail!)

Sea slugs are found mainly in the Red Sea and Indian and western Pacific Ocean.

How do sea slugs differ from to land slugs?

Sea slugs belong to a completely different order of animals to slugs, called Nudibranchia. Instead of having a pair of lungs, like land slugs, sea slugs breathe through gills arranged in clumps on their backs that look a little bit like plants. Like their land-dwelling relatives, they are slow moving and do not have shells. They have a nasty, poisonous taste and warn predators of this by being among the most brightly colored animals in the sea.

Limpets and whelks

Limpets and whelks are also gastropod mollusks. Like slugs and snails, they have a single body 'space' and their shells are not divided, so they are called 'univalves'. Limpets have a cone-shaped shell, rather than the coiled shell of a whelk, and can be either herbivores or filter feeders, depending on the species. Whelks are scavengers and carnivores. They have a siphon that protrudes from their shells and draws water over their gills. Some have a flap at the back of their shell called an 'operculum' that seals the shell when the animal retreats inside.

▶ What is an oyster drill?

An oyster drill is a type of predatory sea snail, much like the New England dog whelk or the veined rapa whelk. Oyster drills attack their prey by climbing onto their shells and drilling a small hole into them. Oysters cannot move so, once the slow process has started, there's no escape. After the hole is made, they insert their proboscis and use the toothed 'radula' to scrape the prey into pieces to be sucked up and eaten.

 *Oyster drills also have a large, muscular foot with which they grip their victims.*

◀ When do common limpets eat?

These conical-shelled limpets live in colonies on rocky shores. Because the seashore rocks on which they live are often left exposed at low tide, they need a firm grip to hang on until the tide returns. When high tide arrives, limpets relax the gripping muscles of their foot so they can graze the rocks for the algae. They will travel up to 3 feet 3 inches/1 meter from their home but, as the tide goes out, they return to exactly the same spot to re-attach themselves and wait until it's safe to eat again.

 *Often unseen, the feet of common limpets can be green-gray, yellow or even orange.*

▶ How do veined rapa whelks leave no marks on clams?

Originally confined to seas near Japan, the rapa whelk is now found much further afield, along the west Atlantic coast. It is a hungry feeder on other mollusks such as oysters, clams and mussels, which it drills or rasps open. It attacks bivalves by rasping along the hinge that joins the two sides of the shell together, so that they fall open, allowing the whelk to suck out and feast on the soft body inside. Once the whelk has finished its meal, it spits out the empty shells.

 *The rapa whelk reproduces by laying a mat of 130 or more egg cases on the seafloor.*

How often can whelks lay their eggs? Up to 10 times a season.

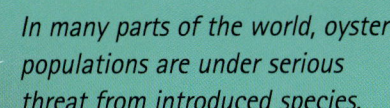 *In many parts of the world, oyster populations are under serious threat from introduced species.*

Why are slipper limpets dangerous to oysters?

Slipper limpets attach themselves to rocks, pebbles, or other shells, and feed by filtering edible material from the water. Slipper limpet young, or larvae, settle to the bottom and attach themselves to the rocks or shells of other animals. The larvae can make 'chains' of limpets, several inches thick. These can entirely cover an oyster bed so that the limpets both starve oysters and smother them by sheer weight of numbers.

Conches, cowries and cone shells

Conches, cowries and cone shells are another group of gastropod mollusk. Like limpets and whelks, they live in the sea and have gills so they can breathe underwater. Like a snail, they have a shell, often coiled into a tube with an opening at one end that may be partly sealed by a type of trap door. They also have two quite well developed eyes, sometimes at the base of a tentacle. In most species the sexes are separate, but reproduction outside of the body is also known.

▼ How do textile cones hunt?

Unlike most mollusks, which are harmless, a number of cone shells, including the textile cone, are poisonous. Like most other mollusks, it hides by day and forages for food at night. It mostly feeds on other mollusks, hunting them down using its sense of smell. When it closes in, it extends a proboscis and explores the other shell, looking for the opening. Once it is found, it pushes it in until it touches flesh, at which point it fires one of its poison-laced, harpoon teeth, which remain attached to it by a thread. Once its victim's body relaxes, it reels it in to eat.

The textile cone's venom is harmful to humans and can cause death within minutes.

How many eggs can a queen conch lay? Females lay over 300,000 eggs!

Humans used to make weapons and tools out of the queen conch's strong shell.

How big is a queen conch?

The queen conch is a large gastropod mollusk, weighing about 4lbs 6oz/2kg – the size and weight of a bowling ball. It is protected by its large shell and a special hard plate that it can clamp shut or use to drag itself around. Although large, it is a gentle creature that feeds mainly on seaweed in the Caribbean Sea. Unfortunately, its shell is one of the reasons it is endangered: people have collected them as souvenirs. They can grow up to 10 inches/ 25 centimeters long and their shells are spiraled with points.

▶ What do cowrie shells look like?

Cowries have egg-shaped shells with a narrow opening. The tiger cowrie is one of the most common and can be found in a majority of tropical waters. The different patterns on the shells are largely decided by genetics, but they can show other things too. If a cowrie moves to an area where conditions differ from the usual conditions the species inhabits, its shell often reflects this in extremely interesting ways. For example, an excess of nickel or zinc in the water can produce extra dark pigmentation. Extra iron can produce rusty colors, and various other elements produce other colors and effects.

 *Cowrie shells are often shiny and porcelain-like because they are covered and protected by a thin body layer called a mantle.*

Do all cowries live on their own?

Unlike most other cowries, the Arabian cowrie likes company and is often found in pairs. They usually live in dark places, such as under large slabs of dead coral, under rocks or in caves where they are protected from the sunlight and predators, such as fish that hunt them during the day. Arabian cowries are night-feeders, feasting on algae and sponges. They are more abundant in areas of the sea that are just below the low-tide level, and on or around coral reefs, rather than in deeper waters.

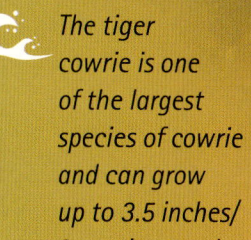 *The tiger cowrie is one of the largest species of cowrie and can grow up to 3.5 inches/ 9 centimeters long.*

25

Bivalves

There are about 15,000 species of bivalves, which include scallops, clams, oysters and mussels. Bivalves are mollusks that have a shell, or valve, on each side of their body which they can close together. Many also have a 'foot' with which they move themselves around. Most bivalves live in the sea. They are 'filter feeders', which means they feed by filtering food particles from the water around them. Some attach themselves to rocks under the water, while others bury themselves on the seabed.

 *Scallop numbers are declining due to worsening water quality. Run-off from land and anti-fouling paints from boats kill the bivalves.*

▲ How do scallops swim?

Scallops propel themselves through the water by opening and closing their shells in a kind of clapping motion. Like oysters, scallops have a strong muscle that holds the two halves of their shell together. This muscle is bigger in scallops like the great scallop because it gets a workout whenever the animal swims. Scallops usually swim away from danger. The edges of their shells are rimmed with a fringe of tentacles and lots of tiny eyes, which are constantly looking for predators.

 *On the black market, giant clam shells are sold as expensive decorations and ornaments.*

How big is the giant clam?

The giant clam is the largest living bivalve. It can weigh more than 400lbs/180kg, or more than a pair of large men, and measure as much as 5 feet/1.5 meters across. As an adult, it remains fixed in one place. Its shell rim is home to a type of algae. During the day, the clam opens so that the algae can receive the sunlight they need to photosynthesize. In return, the clam gets some of its food from them.

Mussels attach themselves to rocks with numerous threads that they produce. They live in clusters of many hundreds.

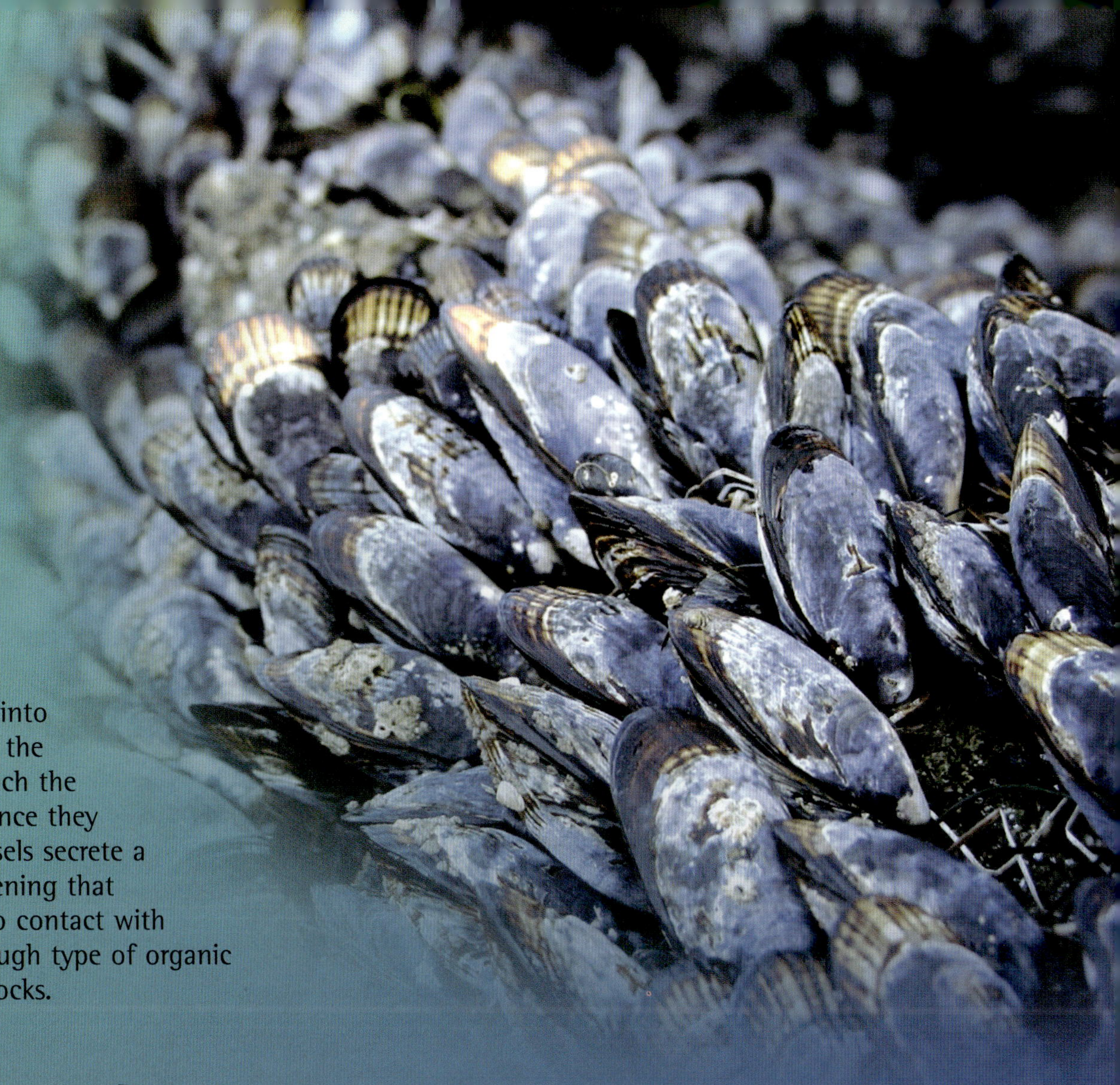

▶ How do mussels move?

Like many bivalves, mussels pull themselves along using a large organ called a 'foot'. They do this by stretching the foot out through an opening in their shell and digging it into the ground. The 'foot' then swells at the end making a type of an anchor, which the mussel uses to pull itself forwards. Once they have found a permanent home, mussels secrete a thick solution through the shell's opening that hardens gradually when it comes into contact with seawater. This forms an extremely tough type of organic cement that secures the mussels to rocks.

How many eyes does a scallop have? Some have over 100.

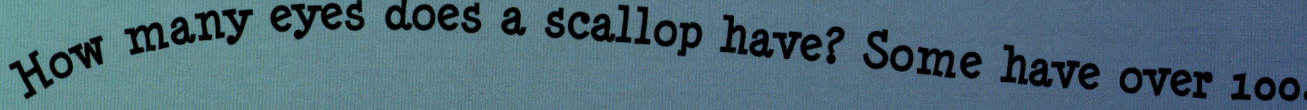

▼ How do oysters breathe?

Oysters breathe in a similar way to fish, using their gills to extract oxygen from the water. They can also use their gills to trap food particles. Oysters have a very hard shell, and strong muscles are used to hold the shell closed. Young oysters are free-swimming in their larval stage, but soon attach themselves to a stationary object, on which they will stay for the rest of their lives.

Oysters are useful in fighting pollution as they help keep water clean. They can filter up to 10.5 pints/ 5 liters of water an hour.

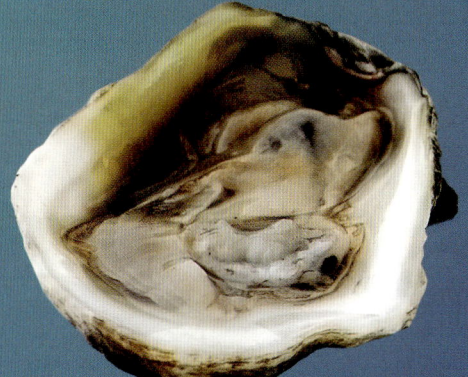

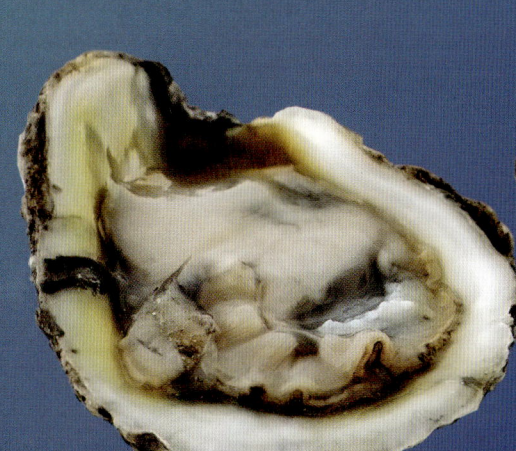

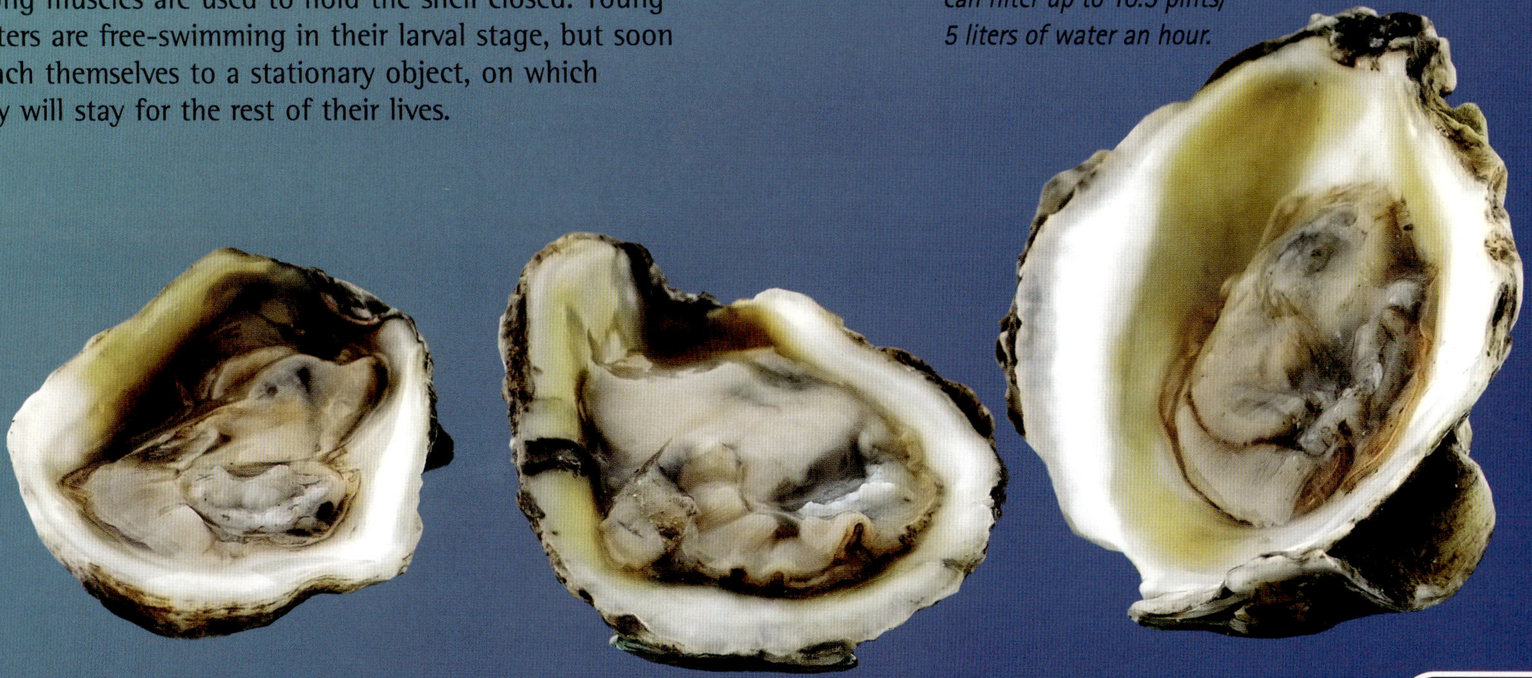

Squid and octopuses

Squid, cuttlefish and octopuses are specialized mollusks known as 'cephalopods'. They are the only invertebrates to have filled the same niche as fish. Unlike most other mollusks, octopuses and squid have no external shell. Squid have an internal shell and have 10 suckered legs. Octopuses have no shell at all and have 8 legs, or tentacles. Both have a beak-like mouth and highly developed senses, with sophisticated eyes that are similar to those belonging to mammals.

Blue-ringed octopuses have two separate poison glands - one to attack prey and the other for defense.

▼ How do reef squid move?

Like all cephalopods, the reef squid moves using jet propulsion. It sucks water in and jets it out again, propelling itself in the opposite direction. The Caribbean reef squid is often found on shallow reefs, and is not scared of divers. Their bodies are broad and less streamlined than many other squids, so they aren't quite as nimble. They are a mottled green-brown on one side with lighter coloring on the other as camouflage.

▲ Are blue-ringed octopuses dangerous?

They are very dangerous – they are the most deadly of all cephalopods to humans. The greater blue-ringed octopus carries enough venom to kill 26 adult humans in minutes – and it is only about the size of a golf ball! This poison is more potent than any poison found in land animals. Luckily, it is not aggressive and will only sting in self-defense. Large shining blue rings cover its surface and they light up when it is alarmed.

How brainy is an octopus?

Cephalopods have the largest brains of all the invertebrates, and the common octopus has one of the largest brain-to-body size ratios, making it the cleverest invertebrate known. Scientists have conducted tests that prove its ability to learn complex signs to get food. Its brainy behavior in the wild includes using its tentacles to search crevices and rocks to find crabs and other small animals. It feeds by drawing food close with its suckered arms and biting its prey with its beak-like mouth.

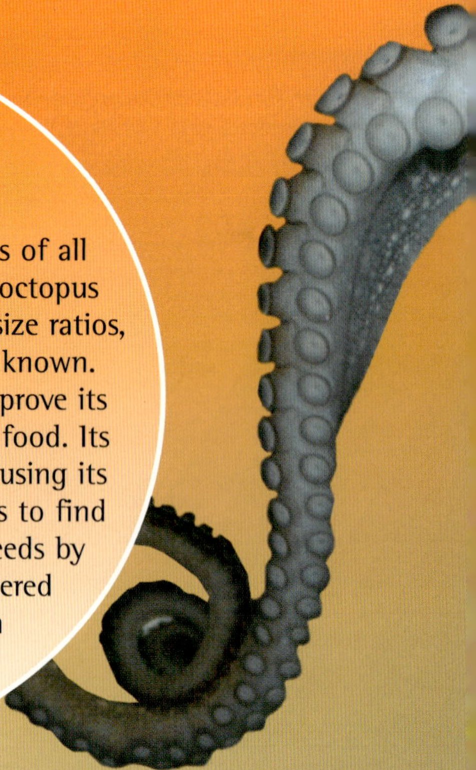

Reef squid can communicate through changing the color of their skin.

28

No one has seen a giant squid in its natural habitat as it lives at such great depths.

Does anything eat giant squid?

Giant squid, and other deep sea squid, are a significant part of a sperm whale's diet. Dramatic underwater battles take place, and sperm whales may be permanently scarred by these encounters as the squid fights back and tries to escape. The giant squid used to be thought of as the largest invertebrate of all, reaching a length of up to 55 feet/16.7 meters and weighing about 2 tons. However, scientists in New Zealand have recently caught a larger squid, that wasn't even fully-grown. They have called it the 'colossal' squid. Like the giant squid, it has a large beak for biting prey, but also swivelling hooks on the end of its tentacles. It could grow to well over 82 feet/25 meters in length.

For how long does a blue-ringed octopus live?

They are not long-lived, averaging just 2 years.

Common octopuses are usually solitary and defend their territories from others.

Krill, shrimp and lobsters

Krill, shrimp and lobsters are all types of crustacean. 'Krill' means 'fish food' in Norwegian and they are a very important source of food for many sea animals including whales, birds and seals. Krill feed on algae, which they collect with the fine hairs covering their legs. Lobsters and shrimp are both decapods, which means '10 legs'. Lobsters also have one pair of legs that are enlarged pincers or claws. Krill, shrimp and lobsters all have elongated abdomens, rather than the rounder bodies of crabs.

If damaged, lobsters are able to regenerate certain body parts like some other crustaceans.

▼ What do harlequin shrimp eat?

The spectacularly patterned harlequin shrimp has a very specific diet: sea stars. Harlequin shrimp find their prey by scent. Once located, harlequin shrimp prise its arms from the rock. They then co-operate to turn the sea star over, which disables it. This allows them to feed on its delicate tube feet, starting at the tips and working inwards. Harlequin shrimp may even feed the sea star prey, keeping it alive so that they can dine on it later.

How far do lobsters travel?

Atlantic lobsters migrate from deeper waters, where they shelter from winter storms, to shallow sand banks where the females dig nests in the sand for their eggs. The journey can cover some 93 miles/150 kilometers and take a month. Lobsters are mainly nocturnal and rely on touch and vibrations rather than vision. Bristles on the body and legs also act as chemical sensors. They are scavengers but also eat seaweed, live fish, small mollusks and other bottom-dwelling invertebrates.

When harlequin shrimp encounter a mate, they stay together for life.

How long do lobsters live for? Some lobsters may live for 50-100 years.

▶ How do red mysid shrimp defend themselves?

When attacked by a predator, red mysid shrimp spit out a bright fluid. This fluid is made up of chemicals that react with each other to produce light, in a process called 'bioluminescence'. The flash of light distracts the predator in the dark of the ocean, giving the shrimp a chance to escape. Despite their spectacular color, mysid shrimp are well camouflaged at the depths at which they live. In the murky light, red appears as a black color, making them shadowy.

The brilliant red coloration of red mysid shrimp looks bright when illuminated but actually works as efficient camouflage in the sea's depths, where light cannot reach.

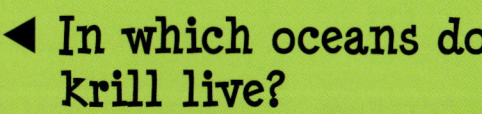

◀ In which oceans do krill live?

Krill live in all the oceans of the world. Antarctic krill are the basis of the whole Southern Ocean food web and support large populations of fish, whales, seals and sea birds. They have a total weight (or 'biomass') of between 100 and 800 million tons, which makes them one of the most abundant animals on the planet.

One krill swarm observed in 1981 is thought to have weighed 10 million tons.

31

Crabs

Crabs are also decapods, meaning they have ten legs. As with lobsters, four pairs are for walking and one pair is for fighting, mating displays and feeding. Like all arthropods, crab bodies are usually covered with a hard coating called an exo – or 'outside' – skeleton. A crab's abdomen is tucked away, giving them a rounder body shape. The abdomen is also narrower in males than in females. Crabs are omnivorous, and eat algae, worms, mollusks, bacteria, fungi and carrion.

Fully-grown female pea crabs can sometimes grow too large to escape the shells in which they live and are imprisoned for the rest of their lives.

▲ Are pea crabs really the size of peas?

They certainly are, but they can grow as large as a broad bean. Pea crabs live in the shells of oysters, cockles and mussels, moving in uninvited for protection. For this reason they are also called 'oyster crabs', although they are found mainly in mussels. They can cause damage to the breathing apparatus of their hosts by occasionally taking a hungry nibble at their gills, and they also steal their host's food to survive. The pea crab is found from southern Scandinavia to western Africa, and throughout the Mediterranean.

▼ Where do hermit crabs get their shells?

Despite their name, hermit crabs aren't true crabs but are instead close relatives. They do not grow their own hard casings like other crabs, so use other empty shells (often mollusk or snail shells) and structures for protection, moving into larger shells as they grow. They move by dragging their shell along the ground with their legs and retreat into it when threatened.

Hermit crabs live in a variety of habitats - some live on land, while others live in the sea.

The common shore crab is a very aggressive species, often fighting with its own kind.

▶ Which crab lives in a rock pool?

Common shore crabs live in waters up to about 197 feet/60 meters deep, but are often found in salt marshes, estuaries and rock pools. Common shore crabs eat worms, small snails, other smaller crabs, algae, carrion or dead animals, mollusks and whatever else they can find. It is more often young or immature common shore crabs that inhabit rock pools.

How much crab do we eat? Over 1.5 million tons a year.

How big is a Japanese spider crab?

Fully grown, the Japanese spider's legspan can be as large as 13 feet/4 meters, which is as long as a car, but it only weighs 44lbs/20kg. It is the largest of all the crabs. These spider crabs live at depths of up to 984-1,310 feet/ 300-400 meters at the bottom of the Pacific Ocean. Japanese spider crabs have orange bodies and their legs are thin with white spots. Despite its huge and fearsome appearance it is fairly docile. This makes them easy to catch and eat and they are under threat from humans.

The Japanese spider crab is a very old species of crab, and it is often referred to as a living fossil.

Centipedes and millipedes

Centipedes and millipedes are arthropods with long, segmented bodies and many legs. Centipedes are predators that hunt using their claws and strong jaws that can inject poison into their prey. They are also flatter-bodied than the rounder-shaped millipedes. Millipedes are not predators but vegetarians, eating rotten or fresh plants. Each segment of a centipede has one pair of legs, while each segment of a millipede has two pairs. Millipedes therefore often have more legs than centipedes, but always less than the 1,000 in their name.

▼ How do millipedes defend themselves?

Although it is large, the giant millipede, like all millipedes, is quite slow and cannot bite or sting. So, a millipede's hard exoskeleton is the first method of defense: many smaller predators cannot pierce it with their jaws. Also, to protect their softer undersides, giant millipedes roll up into a ball and tuck in their legs. Some also secrete toxic substances from glands along the sides of their bodies or the middle of their backs. Some can even produce hydrogen cyanide gas!

The giant millipede coils tightly to defend itself from attack.

The giant centipede's body is made of between 20 and 23 segments and it has around 40-46 legs.

◀ Can centipedes really eat bats?

The giant centipede does. It is the largest centipede in the world and can grow longer than 13 inches/33 centimeters. To hunt bats, giant centipedes crawl into caves and dangle themselves from the ceiling. They then catch them as they fly by and disable them with their strong venom. They can also eat other larger animals such as lizards, frogs, birds and mice. The giant centipede lives in South America and the Caribbean.

Millipedes have blunt heads to help them push through the leaf litter.

How do millipedes walk?

Millipedes walk by lifting each pair of legs at a time – it looks like they are moving along in a wave. Like centipedes, their eyesight is very poor and they sense their way by regularly tapping their antennae on the ground ahead of them. They have special hairs on the second or third pair of legs to keep the antennae clean. Millipedes are 'detritivores', which means they eat rotting wood and leaves collected on the ground, and so play a part in nature's recycling process.

How many legs does a millipede have?
The largest number is 750, but most have between 80 and 400.

Centipedes can have up to 170 legs, although some just have 30.

▶ Which centipedes live under rocks?

Common European centipedes are often found under rocks. They are chestnut-brown in color and feed on insects, spiders and other small invertebrates, including other centipedes. An adult is about 1 inch/2.5 centimeters long with around 30 legs. These centipedes' eyesight is poor so they rely on their antennae to find their way around. They can crawl backwards as well as forwards and locate their food, as well as each other, by smell.

Springtails, silverfish, thrips and lice

Springtails, silverfish, thrips and lice are unrelated invertebrates that are all generally very small – thrips are one of the tiniest flying insects. Springtails can jump to escape predators, but silverfish and lice cannot jump or fly at all. Some of these insects do not have to mate to reproduce and, after they hatch from eggs, their young alter shape very little before they become fully grown adults. Because of this, they are described as being more primitive insects. Lice eat molds or plants or are parasites that feed on a host's blood. Thrips, silverfish and springtails eat a variety of different types of food and some can be pests to humans.

So far, around 5,000 species of thrip have been described.

▲ How do thrips fly?

For thrips (also called 'thunderbugs'), flying can be difficult. They overcome this by having narrow wings fringed with small hairs, making their wings lighter and more flexible than a solid wing. They cannot launch themselves by beating their wings, however, so they jump to take off. Because of their size, they risk drowning when it rains, and it is thought that the air movement caused by the falling raindrops actually moves them out of the way. Thrips are vegetarians, eating the juice of fruit, leaves and pollen.

◀ How do head lice stick to hair?

Head lice have two strong front legs and six claws that they use for clamping hold of hairs, making them difficult to scratch or brush out. The human head louse is the most common species of human louse and they are mainly attracted to cleaner hair, as it is easier for them to clamber around in. They are transmitted by contact and are often passed from one head to another when children's heads touch during play. They stick their white eggs on strands of hair and it is these, or the empty eggshells, often called 'nits', that are usually seen on a head.

The tops of head louse eggs pop off when they are ready to hatch and the louse crawls out.

▶ How do springtails jump?

Springtails have a peg at their rear that is folded beneath the body under tension. It is held in place by a type of clasp that releases when they feel threatened, flinging them into the air. Springtails are found in decaying plant material on soil. They are detritivores, which means they help break down discarded, decaying material, creating soil. They can be found anywhere that soil occurs and in huge numbers. In fact, they are one of the most numerous animals on the planet.

Some springtails are pests that can damage crops, but most are vital for the production of soil.

How long do head lice live?

Several weeks, but only 48 hours if away from a human head.

Silverfish are thought to have existed for over 300 million years.

What do silverfish look like?

Silverfish have many silver, scaly body plates arranged in a row that is flexible and allows them to wriggle into the small damp, dark places in which they live. They are nocturnal and like humid, warm environments. Silverfish eat starchy foods like flour, bread, paper and even glue, hair and dandruff. They can cause annoyance by damaging books or textiles.

Dragonflies

There are about 5,300 species of dragonfly in the world today. They can be split into two smaller groups: 2,900 species of 'true dragonflies', and 2,700 species of 'damselflies'. Both can be recognized by their two pairs of large, veined, independent wings and pairs of large, compound eyes (which are large eyes made of lots of tiny eyes). They are the largest eyes of all insects. Dragonflies eat mosquitoes, midges and other small insects like flies, bees and butterflies, but some larvae eat larger prey such as small fish.

Why are hawker dragonflies called hawkers?

It is due to their fidgety, 'hawking' flight. Like other dragonflies, they can beat both pairs of their wings separately, which helps them to hover and move sideways. They rarely settle, but do sometimes hang from branches to rest. Hawker dragonflies are common worldwide. The American name for hawker dragonflies is 'darner'. This is because their bodies look like sewing needles used to darn cloth.

▼ What is different about damselflies?

Like the emerald damselfly, all damselflies are generally slimmer and daintier than 'true dragonflies'. This is why they are called 'damsels' – which is a word for a young lady. The eyes of damselflies are more widely separated, some almost on short stalks, whereas the eyes of dragonflies meet on the tops of the head, which can make them look a bit like helicopters. Damselflies usually fly more slowly and hold their wings up when at rest, whereas dragonflies flatten them out to the sides.

The design of a dragonfly's wings allows it to fly backwards and sideways as well as forwards.

Many species of damselfly are under threat as their water-based breeding habitats disappear.

Which dragonfly is the oldest?

The petal tails are the oldest type of true dragonfly still living – their fossils date back to over 150 million years ago. They are called petal tails because the enlarged parts of the males' bottoms look like petals. There are only 11 types of petal tail but one, the giant petal tail, is the largest of all true dragonflies, with a wingspan of over 6.5 inches/16.5 centimeters. Dragonflies breed in swampy and boggy areas and rarely leave their breeding ground.

The ancestors of dragonflies date back over 300 million years – they are one of the oldest types of insects in the world.

How fast is a dragonfly?
The top speed of a dragonfly can be between 19 and 38 miles/30 and 60 kilometers an hour.

▶ What does a baby dragonfly look like?

Their appearance can differ greatly from species to species. Generally, baby dragonflies (called 'larvae') live underwater and breathe with small gills. To feed, they ambush their prey by hiding in silt or plant material in ponds and attacking what comes near. Some, like the brown hawker larvae, even attack and eat small fish such as sticklebacks.

From egg to death, the lifecycle of some species of dragonfly can be as long as six or seven years.

Termites and earwigs

Termites are insects that live in large colonies like ants, and some bees and wasps, although they are unrelated. Unlike termites, earwigs are solitary animals. They do demonstrate some social behavior, however: they care for their young and build small nests for themselves. Earwigs are mostly herbivores, and hide in dark recesses during the day and become active at night. Although they are not really related, both termites and earwigs are grouped with winged insects known as 'neopterans'. This is because some species have working wings, others have wings that have shrunk and no longer work, or which they do not use.

▶ How large are termite nests?

Some of the most impressive nests are those made on grassland and they can reach huge proportions, like the nest of the fungus growing termites of Africa. These nests can reach heights of over 23 feet/7 meters – nearly the height of a house! The nests are built out of mud and saliva with a long central chimney that draws air through the nest to keep it cool, preventing the nest from overheating in the hot African sun.

What's magnetic about magnetic termites?

Australian magnetic termites are so named because, when building their nests on dry grassland, they align them in a north-south direction. The reason for this seems to be for temperature control. If the wedge-shaped nests are laid out in the right direction, the flat face is exposed to morning and evening sun, helping to keep the colony warm during the coolest parts of the day. Also, at midday, when the nest could be in danger of overheating in Australia's high temperatures, the sun only beats down on the small surface of the top edge.

Magnetic termites are also known as compass termites.

▼ How do earwigs care for their young?

Common earwigs make nest cavities in the soil under bark or rocks to protect their eggs. If the eggs are disturbed the female earwig scurries around picking them up in her jaws and putting them all back together in one place. She also cleans the eggs carefully, removing fungus or debris. When the young hatch, she feeds them on regurgitated food she collects on short trips during the night and does so for about two weeks until they leave.

Ignore the tall tales told about earwigs – they do not climb into your ear and bite you!

Termites reach very high numbers aided by their social lifestyle. A single colony can house 7 million termites.

How large does a termite queen grow?
Some can swell up to over 5 inches/13 centimeters in length!

Once she has found a nest, the queen termite bites off her wings.

How does a termite nest work?

The termite colony is founded by a mating king and queen termite and mating continues after the nest has been chosen. The queen termite's body then grows huge and distorted to many times its original size and she becomes an egg-laying machine. The first eggs to hatch become 'workers' that forage for food, take care of the young and begin to build a bigger nest. When enough workers have been born, 'soldiers' are produced whose only job is defending the colony.

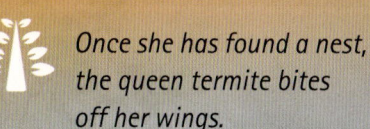

Crickets and grasshoppers

Although many of them are wingless, those grasshoppers that do have wings have two pairs. The front wings are narrower and harder at the base than the back wings. They have large compound eyes and antennae, and their hind legs are enlarged for jumping. They produce sound (known as 'stridulation') by rubbing their wings or their legs against each other or on rows of corrugated bumps. Most lay their eggs in the ground or on vegetation. These eggs hatch into young wingless nymphs that resemble the adults – at this stage they are often called 'hoppers'.

▶ What is different about mole crickets?

Mole crickets spend most of their lives underground. Because of this, and the fact that, like many crickets, they are nocturnal, they are rarely seen. They live in extensive tunnel systems built using shovel-like forelimbs that are well adapted for burrowing under agricultural fields, lawns and golf courses where they are commonly considered pests. Mole crickets do not have the small eyes and poor eyesight of the mammals they are named after. Instead, they have large beady eyes needed for flying around at night in the breeding season when they might fly as far as 5 miles/ 8 kilometers looking for a mate.

In certain parts of the globe, mole cricket numbers are declining due to soil erosion and habitat destruction.

◀ When do locusts swarm?

Locusts are a type of grasshopper. They can breed rapidly under suitable conditions and it is when their population reaches a certain level in one area that they form into swarms and move, or migrate, looking for more food. When they are young they are called 'nymphs' and they form 'bands'. It is the winged adults that form the swarms, but both can travel large distances, destroying huge quantities of crops. The migratory locust is the most common locust species in the world. It lives throughout Africa, Asia and Australia. It used to be common in Europe but is now much rarer.

One of the largest locust swarms recorded contained 40,000 million individuals.

▶ How do crickets chirp?

It is the male cricket that makes the chirping sound. There are two types – the 'calling' and the 'courting' songs. The calling song is much louder and is for attracting females and driving away other males. The courting song is used when a female cricket is near, and is much quieter. Male wings have 'teeth' or 'ridges' and 'scrapers' on them. When they are rubbed together, it makes a chirp in the same way as when you run your nail along a comb. This sound-producing action is called 'stridulation' and the song is different depending on the species of the cricket and the temperature of their environment.

To hear mating calls, crickets and grasshoppers have ears located on their knees, just below the joint of the front legs.

How far can a grasshopper jump? Between 20 and 80 times its own length (which is like a human jumping about 1.5 soccer fields).

A grasshopper has 900 different muscles, compared to 792 in humans.

Can you eat grasshoppers?

In many parts of the world, such as Asia and Africa, grasshoppers and crickets are considered very tasty and are often fried up and eaten as a tasty snack or part of a main dish. However, one group it would not be a very good idea to eat are the 'gaudy grasshoppers'. They are called gaudy because of their bright colors warning predators that they are poisonous to eat. The strangest of the gaudy grasshoppers is the milkweed grasshopper of South Africa. It can froth a large amount of foam from its back legs as a warning if it feels threatened, along with a bad smell.

Cockroaches and mantids

Cockroaches have flattened, oval-shaped bodies, chewing mouths, down-turned legs and long antennae. Most species also have wings but often prefer to scuttle around on the ground. They are one of the most ancient insects on the planet and are great survivors. Slower-moving mantids are easily identified by their raised front legs, especially adapted for catching prey, and their compound eyes that are set high on either side of a highly manoeuvrable triangular-shaped head.

▼ Do cockroaches live in families?

The young of many species of cockroach, such as the American cockroach, do stick together in family groups. It is because they eat wood. Wood is hard to digest, and cockroaches have a special type of micro-organism that lives in their guts that helps them with breaking it down. Young cockroaches are born without this, however, and so must get their own. They usually do this by eating the skins and gut lining left behind by older cockroaches when they shed their casings. Adult cockroaches don't shed their skins, so newly-hatched cockroaches have to hang around their older brothers and sisters to pick up these digestive helpers.

Do cockroaches stink?

Many do – some species leave an unpleasant smell behind them after feeding. One, however, called the stinking cockroach, or the Florida woods roach, uses bad smells as a defense. When surprised or threatened, it releases a foul-smelling spray which can irritate human skin. It lives in central and southern Florida in America and lives in dead logs, tree stumps, limestone rock holes, and piles of firewood. When not defending itself from attackers, however, it actually smells like maraschino cherries!

Cockroaches can live for two to three weeks with no food and water, and up to 42 days without food.

How long have cockroaches been on earth? For at least 340 million years!

The front legs of a praying mantis strike out in a fraction of a second.

▶ How do mantids hunt?

Mantids are ambush predators, meaning they lie in wait for their prey and surprise it. Rather than lurking underneath a leaf or flower for their prey and striking upwards, which can be difficult and lead to mistakes, flower mantids improve their chances by actually sitting on the flowers themselves, taking advantage of their attractive properties for insects. This mantid has pink arms and a pink abdomen of an identical shade to the flower, and the thighs of its two back pairs of legs are expanded into pink petal shapes.

Mantids only have one ear and often cannot tell which direction a sound is coming from.

Do female praying mantises really eat their mates?

It's true that male praying mantises can risk being killed and eaten when they attempt to mate with females. They are smaller than the females, so they can be easily caught or wounded by their sharp front legs. Cannibalism isn't common and only happens when the female is hungry, and is probably due to mistaken identity. The male must always approach with caution, moving slowly while making the right signals with its antennae, legs and abdomen.

Stick and leaf insects

Like mantids, stick and leaf insects often live in the branches of trees and bushes, and are exclusively vegetarian. They tend to be nocturnal feeders as they are slow movers and therefore vulnerable during the daytime. Because of this, many have developed very effective camouflage. Stick insects are 'phasmids', which have elongated bodies that look like twigs or sticks. The main exceptions are the leaf insects that belong to the family 'phyllidae' who have flattened bodies resembling leaves.

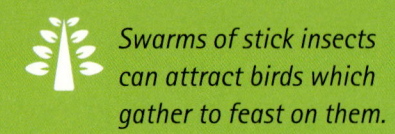

Swarms of stick insects can attract birds which gather to feast on them.

◀ Do stick insects live on their own?

Some species of stick insect can gather in very large numbers and cause quite a lot of damage. One species in Australia, Didymuria violascens, can cause huge problems to eucalyptus trees. In 1963, a vast swarm of these stick insects stripped 650 square miles/1,683 square kilometers of eucalyptus forest – the size of 240 soccer pitches. Eucalyptus trees are not very resilient and can die if stripped of too many leaves.

Do stick insects have any other defenses?

Stick insects don't just rely on camouflage to protect themselves – some have other strategies. The New Guinean stick insect Eurycantha horrida has sharp prickles all over its stout body and legs. If touched, it can use its back legs as a vice to crush its attacker. It can also curve its body around to make itself look like a snake about to attack. Other stick insects mimic scorpions about to strike and some can even spray chemicals backwards over a distance of 16 inches/ 40 centimeters at predators.

There are about 2,500 different species of stick insect.

Can leaf insects fly?

As with many stick insects, the males can fly but the females are flightless. Green Javanese leaf insect, like females have large front wings that lie edge-to-edge on the abdomen. The way they are arranged looks like the vein system on a leaf. Like stick insects, female leaf insects don't always need a male to fertilize them and many let their eggs drop to the forest floor. In some species, eggs resemble seeds, and are collected by ants and housed in their nests.

Fossils of leaf insects have been found that are 47 million years old.

▼ How do stick insects hide themselves?

Stick insects don't always purposefully hide themselves in piles of twigs or undergrowth that looks like them. Instead, the intention of many is to resemble fallen twigs from the rainforest canopy high above. Such debris rains down almost constantly, and the lower leaves on rainforest trees catch them. A stick insect like the bent twig stick insect will often position itself in the middle of the lowest part of the leaf, where these falling twigs would normally rest. If disturbed, many species will simply fall to the floor like a stick to continue the disguise.

Most stick insects sway gently in the breeze to blend in with the rustling leaves around them.

Where do leaf insects live? They live in forests on islands in the South Pacific, and in Africa, Sri Lanka, and parts of northern Australia.

47

True bugs

There are over 67,000 species of true bugs and they can be found in every habitat – gardens, mountains, lakes, rivers and ponds. Many are pests to mankind but even more are helpful, fertilizing plants, or eating dead animals. Bugs belong to an order of animals called 'Hemiptera' from the Greek word meaning 'half-wing' after the way in which some of their wings work. Their most distinctive feature is that they don't have jaws and cannot chew.

▼ Do lantern flies light up at night?

People used to believe that the heads of lantern flies glowed at night. Lantern flies are perhaps the most odd-looking of the world's bugs, especially their heads, which are often adapted in many strange ways. There are 750 species worldwide and they are at their most varied in the rainforests. Most bizarre of all is probably the peanut bug, so named because of its huge head shaped like an unshelled peanut.

Lantern flies feed by sucking the sap from the trunks of trees.

◄ Can true bugs sing?

Not as such, but one sort of bug – the cicada – can certainly make a racket. There are over 2,250 species and it is the males' mating call that makes all the noise. This 'singing' is caused by a rapidly clicking membrane amplified by sacs of air in the body. Some sound like mechanical saws cutting through timber. Cicadas can grow up to 4 inches/ 10 centimeters long, and have big, blunt heads. They can fly with their strong, normally transparent wings.

Cicadas are eaten by people in many parts of the world and sometimes used in Chinese medicines.

◀ What is the largest true bug?

The largest bug is the giant water bug, which can be found all over the world, but mainly in America and Asia. The largest species is the toe-biter which can exceed 5 inches/ 12 centimeters in length. Water bugs hunt small fish, amphibians and crustaceans, lurking motionless at the bottom of freshwater streams or ponds and then pouncing on any prey that comes near. They inject a powerful toxin with their mouthpiece and then suck out the digested insides of their unfortunate victims.

Giant water bug males carry eggs on their back until they hatch.

Which bug's bite is the worst?
The giant water bug - the most painful of all insect bites.

Toad bugs often carry mud or pebbles on their backs, to help with disguise.

Which bug has bulging eyes?

Toad bugs have a warty and crouched appearance and move by hopping, much like the toads they're named after. Also like toads, they often have very flattened faces and large bulging eyes on top of their heads. Toad bugs live at the edges of ponds, where they blend in well with the surroundings – they also look like small pebbles. In total, there are around 75 species and they are mainly found all over North and South America.

Lacewings and caddis flies

Both lacewings and caddis flies are part of a large group of flying insects called 'neoptera'. Lacewings are part of an order called 'neuroptera' – or 'net wings' – which includes ant-lions and mantis flies. Caddis flies are 'trichoptera', which means 'hair wings', because their wings have tiny hairs on them. Both neuroptera and trichoptera use both pairs of their wings to fly – the front pair beating slightly before the back pair – and both of these insects go through a complete metamorphosis.

☼ Ant-lions can dig pits up to 3 inches/ 8 centimeters wide and 2 inches/5 centimeters deep – large enough to bury a golf ball.

▼ Are mantid flies related to praying mantises?

They are not related but they behave like them and look very similar. Mantid flies catch their prey with their spiny front legs and they often hold these up in a similar way to praying mantises. They often hunt and chase down their food of moths, caterpillars, spiders and other insects, and their larvae are also predators that eat bee or wasp larvae and spider eggs. Mantid flies are usually green or brown in color, but some can be yellow or even pink.

▲ Where do ant-lions live?

Ant-lions live all over the world in sandy places on the edges of coniferous forests where they mate as adult flies. The name ant-lion refers to the larvae. They live in sandy soil and dig steep pits in which they rest at the bottom, leaving their jaws exposed. They pick dry, sunny spots sheltered from wind and rain. When an ant falls into the pit, it cannot escape as the sides collapse as it tries to climb out. The ant-lion larvae catch them in their large jaws and feed by sucking them dry.

☼ Mantid fly eggs are green and stalked and are laid in clusters.

▼ **Where do caddis flies lay their eggs?**

Caddis flies lay their eggs on the surface of water or on water plants. The larvae of many species are good builders and construct protective casings out of silk, sand and bits of shell arranged in a spiral. This case is portable, and caddis flies drag it around as they move, holding it in place with a pair of hooked legs. They build new, larger cases as they grow, and then pupate inside the last before emerging as a winged adult. However, some species' larvae are free-swimming predators.

What do lacewings eat?

Lacewings prey on aphids and other soft-bodied insects. The larvae of some species camouflage themselves with the dried carcasses of their prey – this makes them look like small piles of debris. Lacewing larvae have extremely long, slender and obvious jaws (or 'mandibles') that curve forward from the front of the head. These mandibles are tubes that are sunk into the victim's body. The larvae can then suck out the body fluids of their victims as if they were using two drinking straws.

☀ *Caddis fly larvae attach various bits of debris to their silk cases to add to their camouflage.*

☀ *Adult lacewings communicate by vibrating the surface on which they are standing.*

How many aphids can a lacewing larva eat? These predators can feast on up to 50 a day.

51

Flies

Although many bugs have 'fly' as part of their name, flies are actually a completely separate group to other winged insects. The major difference is that they only have one pair of wings. In place of a second pair of hind wings, they have small body parts called 'halteres' that help them balance when they fly. As a result they are very skilful flyers. Nearly all flies feed by sucking up liquids like blood and nectar. Others have a kind of spongy organ that dissolves and absorbs their food.

▼ How do robber flies hunt?

Robber flies are fast flyers that attack and eat other flies and bugs. They have strong legs and can even catch their prey in mid-air. Like most flies, robber flies have two large compound eyes either side of their head but they also have three simple eyes in between these. Robber flies stab their prey with their short proboscis. They then inject a type of saliva containing neurotoxins into it. The toxins cause paralysis, and enzymes in the saliva digest the prey's insides.

Robber flies attack butterflies, moths, beetles, bees, dragonflies, grasshoppers and even some spiders.

Housefly maggots can hatch in less than a day - between 8 and 20 hours after being laid.

▲ How do flies grow?

Flies undergo a complete metamorphosis, from a larval stage as a maggot into an adult fly after pupating – as do butterflies and many other bugs. A number of species of maggot eat rotting meat and dead flesh. Some types of maggots can also be used to treat a wound to prevent it going bad – they eat away all the infected flesh and leave the healthy alone. Maggots are also a useful food for a number of different animals.

What do houseflies eat?

Houseflies eat anything sugary or rotting that they can dab up and absorb with their spongy mouthparts. The housefly is one of the most common insects and has followed humans wherever they have gone. This is because their behavior fits well with human activity: they lay their eggs in all sorts of animal manure and household waste. They are considered a pest as they can carry diseases in their saliva and on their bodies.

Flies can beat their wings hundreds of times a second. Some species manage 1,000.

How long does it take for houseflies to grow from eggs? As little as 12-14 days.

▶ Do all mosquitoes suck blood?

Actually, male mosquitoes feed on the nectar of plants. Female mosquitoes are the ones that suck blood with their sharp mouthparts designed to pierce the skin. They need blood in order to make eggs. They are dangerous, however, because they can carry a number of unpleasant diseases, such as malaria, dengue fever and yellow fever, injected at the same time as they feed. Female mosquitoes lay their eggs on the surface of stagnant water and the larva that hatch – feeds – on animals and plant material before turning into a pupa in which it undergoes a full metamorphosis into an adult.

Mosquitoes' saliva contains an enzyme that prevents the blood from clotting.

Butterflies and moths

Butterflies and moths are different from other flying insects because they are covered in tiny scales. Although they look similar, there are easy ways to tell them apart. Butterflies fly during the day, whereas moths fly at night. Butterfly antennae end in club-like tips, while moth antennae come in a variety of different shapes, none of which end in a club. Butterflies rest with their wings raised while most moths rest with their wings laid flat.

▼ **Do any butterflies migrate like birds?**

Yes, monarch butterflies do. Each generation of monarch butterfly that hatches in Canada is able to find its way to Mexico to roost for the winter, at exactly the same place as generations before them. No one knows quite how they do this. Scientists believe the monarch butterflies use the sun somehow as a compass to help guide them south. They believe that, as with most insect behavior, this information is stored in their genes. But, again, exactly how this works is not known. This is for a scientist in the future to solve!

The migration of monarch butterflies takes them over 2,000 miles/ 3,200 kilometers.

How fast can a death's-head hawkmoth fly? About 25 miles/40 kilometers an hour, but faster in short bursts.

54

Why are tiger moths so brightly colored?

Like many insects, tiger moths use their bright colors to warn predators of danger. These moths taste disgusting and can be slightly poisonous if eaten. Garden tiger moth caterpillars are also known as 'woolly bears' as their bodies are covered with long black hairs. These hairs help protect the young caterpillar, as predators find the furry coats hard to swallow.

Tiger moths can produce high-frequency sounds which jam the sonar system of bats.

The common yellow swallowtail has a wingspan of between 4 and 5 inches/8 and 10 centimeters.

◀ Why do swallowtail butterflies have long tails?

The common yellow swallowtail is widespread throughout Europe and can be found in mountain meadows in Austria, Italy and Spain as well as coastal areas and patches of wasteland. It gets its name from the shape of its wings, which resemble of a swallow's tail. These are also a useful means of defence. It is not uncommon to find them with damaged tails. This is because birds and other predators are fooled into thinking the butterfly is the other way up – the large red spots on its wings look like eyes and the tails look like antennae, giving the false impression of a head and allowing the butterfly vital moments to escape.

▼ How do death's-head hawkmoths get their name?

Death's-head hawkmoths are named after the eerie skull-like pattern on their backs. Some people even believe that it's bad luck for a death's-head hawkmoth to come into your house. Unlike other moths that feed on flower nectar, death's-head hawkmoths ransack bee hives and nests for honey, earning them the nickname 'bee tiger'. Death's-head hawkmoths are strong flyers, spending the summer months in Europe and wintering in Africa. They lay their eggs on potato plants, and their numbers are declining because of insecticides used to protect the plants.

Male death's-head hawkmoths will run and hop around making high-pitched squeaking noises if disturbed.

55

Bees and wasps

Bees and wasps (along with ants) belong to a group called 'hymenoptera' which means 'membrane wings'. Bees and wasps both have four wings that are thin and see-through. They have small hooks joining the back of the front wing to the front of the back wing on each side – these are known as 'married wings'. Bees feed mainly on plants. They have long tongues that they can use to suck up the nectar from flowers. Wasps hunt other bugs, and some are parasitic.

Leafcutter bees are not aggressive and have only a mild sting.

▼ Do all wasps live in hives?

No, many wasps are solitary animals. Sand wasps make single nests in sandy soil. This takes a female most of one day. After inspecting the nest carefully, she goes hunting. Once she catches her caterpillar prey, she stings it several times and then drags or flies it back to the nest and lays eggs on it. When fully stocked with one or more caterpillars, the female seals the entrance with soil. When the eggs hatch, the young have a fresh supply of food!

▲ How do leafcutter bees build their nests?

Like most bees, the female leafcutter bee is solitary and builds individual nests. She does this by cutting an almost circular chunk from rose leaves. Then she carries the leaf segment back to a nest hole, often in a hollow plant stem or among the roots of cactus plants. She constructs a small chamber by sticking a number of leaf segments together, using their sticky sap. She stocks each chamber with nectar and pollen gathered from plants and then lays an egg on this food and seals the cell with more leaf fragments. The young leafcutter bee then has food when it hatches.

There are 20 species of sand wasp. Some build decoy nest holes to confuse predators.

▶ Do common wasps build nests?

Yes, common wasps build new nests every year. In spring, fertilized females (or 'queens') start building a new hive with paper made from chewed-up wood. The queen then lays eggs on bits of chewed-up insects in sealed chambers. The eggs hatch and eat the food and become 'workers' that take over foraging for food and building the nest while the queen wasp lays more eggs. At the end of the year, new queens leave the nest with males to mate and then hibernate. Then they start the whole process again the next year.

Common wasp nests can contain up to 10,000 individuals.

How many trips does a honeybee make in a day?

On average, each bee makes about 15 trips a day.

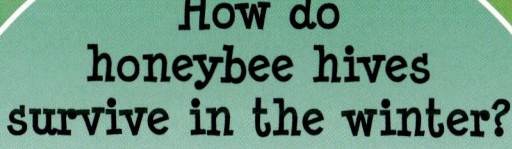

How do honeybee hives survive in the winter?

Colonies of honeybees can survive the winter because they generate warmth in the hive. They do this by contracting the muscles they use for flight but without flapping their wings – this is a lot like humans shivering. Honeybees need a lot of energy to do this, however, so the hive must be well stocked with honey. The honey is stored in hexagonal cells and sealed with bee's wax.

Bees visit hundreds of flowers each day, collecting pollen and fertilizing the plants.

Ants

Although ants are grouped with bees and wasps, there are a few differences. Ants usually have a more varied diet. Most ants are scavengers, searching the environment around them for whatever titbits they come across. Others are purely vegetarian, and some are even aggressive predators that hunt other bugs. Ants are social animals, living in nests or large groups. Their nests can be made from a variety of materials, but ant nests can grow into much larger networks, housing many millions of individuals. Many ants have powerful stings.

Leafcutter ants' nests can be as much as 19 feet 6 inches/6 meters deep.

How large do ant nests grow? One colony of 45,000 connected nests in Japan contained 300 million individuals and 1 million queens!

▲ Why do leafcutter ants cut leaves?

Leafcutter ants live in the rain forests of Central and South America and build large nests underground in which they sleep at night. By day, however, they are hard-working farmers. Worker ants follow scent trails up to the tops of trees and cut pieces of leaf to carry back to the nest. Here, smaller worker ants chew the leaves into a sort of mushy compost on which they grow a fungus. The ants then 'harvest' the fungus for food.

▼ Do all ants live in nests?

Unlike most ants, army ants don't build a permanent nest. Instead, they build temporary camps called bivouacs at the end of each day after searching for food in forests in Central or South America and Africa. Because of their numbers and their powerful jaws, they can kill and eat animals many times larger than themselves, such as mice and small birds. They form the walls of their bivouacs by clinging to each other with their legs.

An army ant colony may contain 500,000 individuals.

How do weaver ants make their nests?

Weaver ants live in tropical Africa, Australia and South East Asia in nests built by pulling leaves together into small chambers. The ants work in teams, as they are not strong enough to move the leaves on their own. When a leaf is close enough together, the ants grab a baby ant, called a 'grub', in their mouths, and push it over the leaf. The grub produces a type of silk that sticks the leaves together.

The difference in size between the smallest and largest weaver ant workers can be as much as tenfold.

▼ Why do wood ants farm aphids?

Wood ants protect aphids – mainly from ladybugs – by positioning themselves around them in trees and on plants while the aphids feed. This is in order to collect the drops of honeydew the aphids make while eating. Wood ants also feed on other small insects, using their strong bites to kill them and drag them back to the nest. They live in nests in the forests, and some gardens, of Europe.

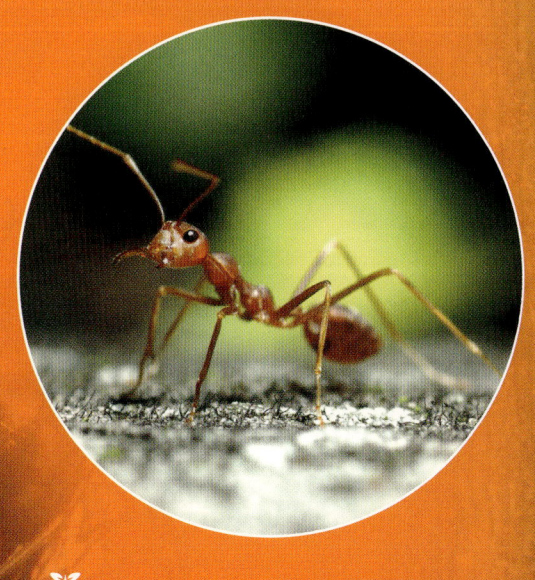

The nests of wood ants can reach up to 5 feet/1.5 meters high – about as tall as a 12-year-old.

Ladybugs, stags and titans

Beetles form the largest order of insects, with well over 350,000 known species. Along with butterflies, bees and flies, they are considered to be one of the 'more advanced' insects, because they undergo a complete transformation between their young (larva) and adult states. Winged beetles' soft hind wings fold under hard, protective front wings that meet and form a straight line down their backs. Their mouthparts are able to bite and chew, rather than being adapted for sucking like those of bugs. With tough, waterproof casings, beetles live all over the world and do many useful jobs.

Titan beetles are quite aggressive, but hiss a warning before attacking.

▼ How many spots does a ladybug have?

It depends on the species – some have as many as 21 spots, others have none at all. There are over 3,400 species of ladybug all over the world, so there are all kinds of possible combinations of red and black, spots or no spots – some are even yellow. Their bold colors warn birds and other predators that these bugs taste bad. Ladybugs feed mainly on aphids, which are harmful to plants, making them very useful around the garden. They are found in meadows, gardens, parks, marshy places and fields all over the world. Ladybugs gather in groups in winter and hibernate among leaf litter.

▲ How big is a titan beetle?

The titan beetle can measure as large as 7 inches/ 18 centimeters from the tip of its hard abdomen to the ends of its powerful jaws, or up to 8 inches/21 centimeters if you include its antennae. It has been reported that it can snap a pencil in its mouth and that it can even cut into human flesh! These huge beetles are only found in and around the Amazonian rainforests in South America. Not much more is known about them, and scientists have yet to find any larvae.

Ladybugs produce unpleasant chemicals from their knee joints to ward off predators.

Despite their ferocious appearance, male stag beetles are not aggressive and will only attack if threatened.

▶ **Why do dung beetles roll piles of poo?**

Although it may seem odd to us, dung beetles are actually very fond of faeces. They spend a lot of time skilfully constructing balls of dung to roll to a nest site so they, and their larvae, can eat it. In this way, these bugs are very useful recyclers, providing a welcome waste-disposal service for other animals. In some species, both the males and females cooperate in constructing one large dung ball. In others, they might build one each. And some build many to stock the nest with. Many varieties are found rolling dung balls of various sizes in North America, Mexico and Africa.

In Australia, dung beetles were imported from Africa to help control flies by recycling the large amount of droppings from cattle.

How long do titan beetles live for? Unfortunately for them, no more than a few weeks in their adult state.

Why do stag beetles have such large jaws?

Male stag beetles have very large jaws. The mouthpart of the female is normally about one-sixth of her size. The males use their large jaws to fight over females and they do battle by trying to force each other off a tree trunk where a female might be likely to lay eggs. Male European stag beetles can measure up to 3 inches/7.5 centimeters long and are found all over Europe. Worldwide, there are more than 1,000 varieties.

61

Fireflies and bombardiers

Three-quarters of the animals on Earth are bugs and the largest group is the beetles. Although 350,000 different species have been found, it is estimated that there could be millions of undiscovered species. They are by far the most varied life form on the planet and, without them, flowers would have more difficulty pollinating and many complex food chains would collapse.

Light made by fireflies is over 30 times more efficient than a 100-watt house lightbulb.

The temperature of the bombardier beetle's explosive mixture of gasses and fluids is hotter than boiling water!

▲ Why don't bombardier beetles explode?

Bombardier beetles defend themselves by squirting a boiling mix of chemicals at their attackers. These chemicals react with air, causing a puff of smoke and a popping sound like a balloon bursting. This spraying is so controlled that it can even aim it, by using a pair of reflectors at the tip of its abdomen. The bombardier beetle stores these chemicals in different parts of its body, only mixing them together when threatened, and using them quickly to avoid injuring itself.

How do fireflies make light?

The light emitted by fireflies is caused by a chemical reaction in their lower abdomens between 'luciferase' and 'luciferin'. This process is called 'bioluminescence'. It is used for attracting or finding mates. Each species of firefly has its own unique flashing patterns, emitted by the males looking for females. Often the females do not fly, but they can flash response patterns for the males to find. Some species of firefly gather in large groups and flash in unison, while others can mimic the patterns of a different species to lure them in before killing them.

▶ Can a Hercules beetle fly?

Although you wouldn't think so looking at it, unbelievably it can! The Hercules beetle is from a family of beetles known as scarabs, which are characterized by stumpy bodies that are often shiny or brightly colored. Scarabs have large horns or jaws, and the Hercules beetle has the largest of all – they are longer than their own bodies. The horns belong to the males of the species, which use them to fight over mates. Although they have smaller horns, the females have a larger body.

The Hercules beetle is the strongest creature for its size – it can carry up to 850 times its own body weight. This is like a human lifting 5 double-decker buses full of people!

How long is a Hercules beetle? It can reach 7.5 inches/19 centimeters.

▶ Are beetles mimics?

Some species of longhorn beetle look like bees and wasps to protect themselves from predators. The bee beetle has a furry coating and buzzes when it flies, just like a medium-sized bumble bee. Also like bees, they are often found on flowers or thistles in June and July, mainly in mountainous areas. Wasp beetles can be found on flowers in May and June, where they feed on nectar. They lay their eggs on sticks and dead wood. Both beetles are found in Europe, with similar species in North America.

The larvae of bee beetles develop in rotting wood, but the adults feed on blossoms.

Sea stars and sea urchins

Sea stars and sea urchins are echinoderms, which means 'spiny-skinned' animals. Their bodies are arranged around five parts, and they all have tube feet. Most sea stars live on open coastal reefs or sheltered waters and have suckers on their feet, while others have points for digging if they live on rocky sand. Sea urchins are separated into 'regular' and 'irregular' types. Regular sea urchins have a rounded internal skeletal shell and live among reefs, rubble, algae beds, and on rocks. Irregular ones live in sand or mud.

How many arms does a sea star have?

Most sea stars, including the common European sea star, have five arms, but some can have as many as 50. Common sea stars come in a variety of colors, though they are mainly orange or reddish-brown. They have a spiny top side and are actually quite agile. They hunt and eat mussels and scallops by walking on top of them and prising them apart, before slipping their stomachs into the shell to digest them where they lie.

▼ Are any sea stars harmful to humans?

Some species of sea star are poisonous enough to cause harm to humans. One of the worst is the crown of thorns sea star of the Indo-Pacific Oceans. It is aggressive looking: its body and up to 23 arms are covered in long, sharp and venomous spines that can cause painful wounds leading to a fever, vomiting or even paralysis. Usually, these sea stars use their poisonous spines as protection from predators such as the puffer fish. The crown of thorns sea star is also a destructive predator on coral and has caused damage to many living coral reefs.

Although the crown of thorns sea star can destroy huge areas of coral reefs, efforts to stop it have increased our knowledge of these habitats.

▶ What is a sand dollar?

The sand dollar is a type of flat sea urchin whose skeletons or 'tests' are often found washed up on shore. They usually live in sand or mud where they can partially bury themselves quickly under the surface. Nearly all sand dollars live in large colonies close to the shore. Some sand dollars move using small spines on their underside. They trap algae in these underside spines and grasp it with raised suckers.

Sand dollars can come in different colors ranging from pink-grey to red or even black.

How many species of echinoderm are there? Roughly 7,000 have been found so far.

Not much detail is known about the life histories of most sea urchins – they are mysterious animals.

▲ Why are sea urchins spiny?

Like many sea urchins, the purple sea urchin's round body is encircled by a large number of spines that protect the animal from predators. In this case, the long and sharp cactus-like spines are colored pink through to purple. This sea urchin holds itself in place with 10 suckered feet arranged in rows on its underside. This is also where the mouth is located, with its five teeth used for scraping algae from rocks.

Like many sea stars, the common sea star can re-grow a leg if it loses one.

Spiders

Spiders are the world's dominant land carnivores. There are close to 40,000 known species and they have successfully occupied nearly every part of the world. All spiders have a pair of hollow fangs through which venom is released. Based on the arrangement of their jaws, spiders are separated into two groups: 'mygalomorphs', which have jaws at the front of their head which strike downwards, and 'true spiders', whose jaws are below the head and strike sideways in a pinching movement.

Trapdoor spiders drag their prey into their underground chambers to dine in peace!

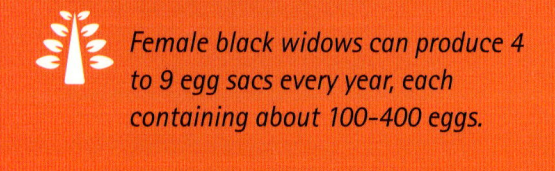

▲ Do all spiders make webs?

Not all spiders make webs, but all produce silk. Many hunt on the ground, like the jumping spiders, and some even build trapdoors. There are many different species of trapdoor spider. They build burrows in firm ground and many of them top them with a silk-hinged lid. Some species build a ring of trip-lines extending from the burrow. These spiders sit and wait, then rush out of their holes to catch passing prey detected through vibrations in the ground.

Female black widows can produce 4 to 9 egg sacs every year, each containing about 100-400 eggs.

◀ Are black widows dangerous?

There are over 30 species of widow spiders, including the red back in Australia. Both the black widow and the red back are mainly black in color, with red on the underside or back of the abdomen to warn off predators. Eating a black widow or red back will normally not kill a predator, such as a spider-eating bird, but it would make it ill enough for them to learn to avoid it in future! They are quite dangerous to humans too. Most people recover from the bite after about a month, but five percent of those bitten die.

▶ Which is the largest family of spiders?

The world's largest family of spiders is the jumping spider, with over 4,000 species worldwide. They are quite small, with large forward-facing eyes. These large eyes enable them to spot prey from a distance of over several inches/centimeters, before stalking it and then leaping on top. Some can give painful bites, with reactions to venom lasting as long as two weeks, but none are fatal or dangerous to humans.

Some jumping spiders can jump 30 times their own body length – that's like jumping over 150 feet/ 46 meters for a man!

Which are the largest spiders?

Tarantulas are the largest spiders in the world. Most live in silk-lined retreats on the ground or on cliff faces or in trees. The largest species has a legspan of 10 inches/ 25 centimeters. Some tarantulas eat small vertebrates such as mice, birds (attacking them in their nests), frogs, lizards and snakes – even poisonous ones. They have clusters of hairs known as 'brushes' on the ends of their legs that help them climb up smooth surfaces.

Is it true that all spiders have 8 eyes?
Most do, but some only have 6.

Tarantulas, like many spiders, cannot see much more than light, darkness, and movement.

Scorpions

Scorpions live all over the world but mostly occur in dry, warm regions. Like spiders, they are arachnids and have eight legs. Scorpions have a pair of venom glands located in the stinger, in the last segment of the tail, which they use mainly for hunting. Scorpion venom is designed to work best against other invertebrates, so most are not harmful to humans. They feed on a variety of insects, and the larger scorpions occasionally feed on vertebrates such as small lizards, snakes and mice.

How do scorpions look after their young?

Unlike spiders, scorpions are born one by one, and the brood is carried on the mother's back until they are old enough to fend for themselves. This is after they have shed their first skin. Depending on the species, sometimes there can be as many as 100 young scorpions to take care of. The emperor scorpion takes especially good care of her babies, and does so for longer than most species.

The emperor scorpion can grow to 7 inches/18 centimeters long and is one of the largest in the world.

How many species of scorpion are there? About 1,200 worldwide.

▶ Are scorpions solitary creatures?

Most are, with one exception: the Arizona bark or crevice scorpion. Although it spends a lot of its time on its own, these scorpions gather in groups of up to 30 in winter to keep warm. They can normally be found scuttling around in rocky areas under boulders, logs, and tree bark. The bark scorpion is good at climbing and is sometimes spotted on the walls of houses in California, Nevada, South Utah, Arizona and South Western New Mexico in America, where it is the most common house scorpion.

The venom of the bark scorpion may cause severe pain and difficulty breathing, but human deaths are rare.

▼ Do you get scorpions in Europe?

The European yellow-tailed scorpion is found in warm European countries such as Italy or Portugal. It is quite small, growing to a maximum length of 2 inches/ 5 centimeters, and eats insects and other small invertebrates. It is expanding its range because of global warming, and colonies have now been found living in the United Kingdom.

Yellow-tailed scorpions' venom is about as potent as a bee sting.

Which is the most venomous scorpion?

The deathstalker scorpion may be the most venomous. Its venom contains a powerful cocktail of a number of neurotoxins. In the wild, it lives in deserts and scrublands across North Africa and the Middle East. Compared to other scorpions it is fairly lightly built, with a long, thin tail, and quite narrow claws, probably because its powerful sting is defense enough. Another contender for the title is the fat-tailed scorpion of North Africa whose venom is similar to cobra's in terms of toxicity.

Sea spiders and horseshoe crabs

Sea spiders are not really spiders at all, but are part of a group of invertebrates with between eight and 12 legs, slim bodies and small heads called 'Pycnogonida', which are only distantly related to arachnids. Likewise, the ten-legged, long-tailed horseshoe crabs are not really crabs but are part of a group of animals called 'Merostomata', which are also distantly related to arachnids. Both of these animals have antennae and bodies that are divided into two parts, and grow by shedding their skins. They are described as 'living fossils' as they are the only surviving relatives of extinct animals.

▼ How do sea spiders survive underwater?

The sea spider has a lot of surface area for its size because of its long legs and slim body. This means that, instead of breathing through a particular organ, like gills, it may just breathe across the walls of its body. They may also dispose of waste materials in the same way. They have a small brain structure and a tube-shaped heart that pulses blood around the body at between 90 and 180 beats a minute. Not much more is known about how their bodies work.

▼ What does a sea spider look like?

As the name suggests, sea spiders look a bit like a spider. They can range in size from the very small, with a legspan of just a few inches/centimeters to the very large with a leg span of 2 feet 6 inches/75 centimeters, such as species of 'colossendeis' sea spiders that live mainly in deep waters. Sea spider bodies are very narrow, often about the width of one of the legs. On its head it has a large proboscis used for piercing and sucking up food. Most sea spiders eat corals, sea anemones and other soft-bodied animals.

It is thought that the sea spiders are the surviving members of a group of animals that died out around 400 million years ago.

There are about 1,000 species of sea spider that have been found and described but there are likely to be many more.

How long do horseshoe crabs live? About 20 years.

What do horseshoe crabs look like?

Most striking are the armor that covers their body and their long spiny tail that helps to steer them in the water. They can reach up to 2 feet/ 60 centimeters long and have five pairs of legs plus a pair of pincers either side of the mouth for picking up food. They have 10 eyes and can even see ultraviolet light. They grow by molting their skins – a male horseshoe will molt 16 times over 9 years and a female 17 times over 11 years. Males are smaller than the females.

▼ What's related to a horseshoe crab?

The horseshoe crab is closely related to a trilobite – an animal that lived over 540 million years ago. There are only four species alive today, and they can be found in the West Pacific and West Atlantic Oceans and the Indian Ocean near Indonesia. They come ashore to breed and are vulnerable to being caught by migrating seabirds, for which they are an important source of food.

If a horseshoe crab flips on its back, it can use its tail or telson to flip it the right way again.

Horseshoe crabs burrow into sand to eat mollusks, worms and other invertebrates.

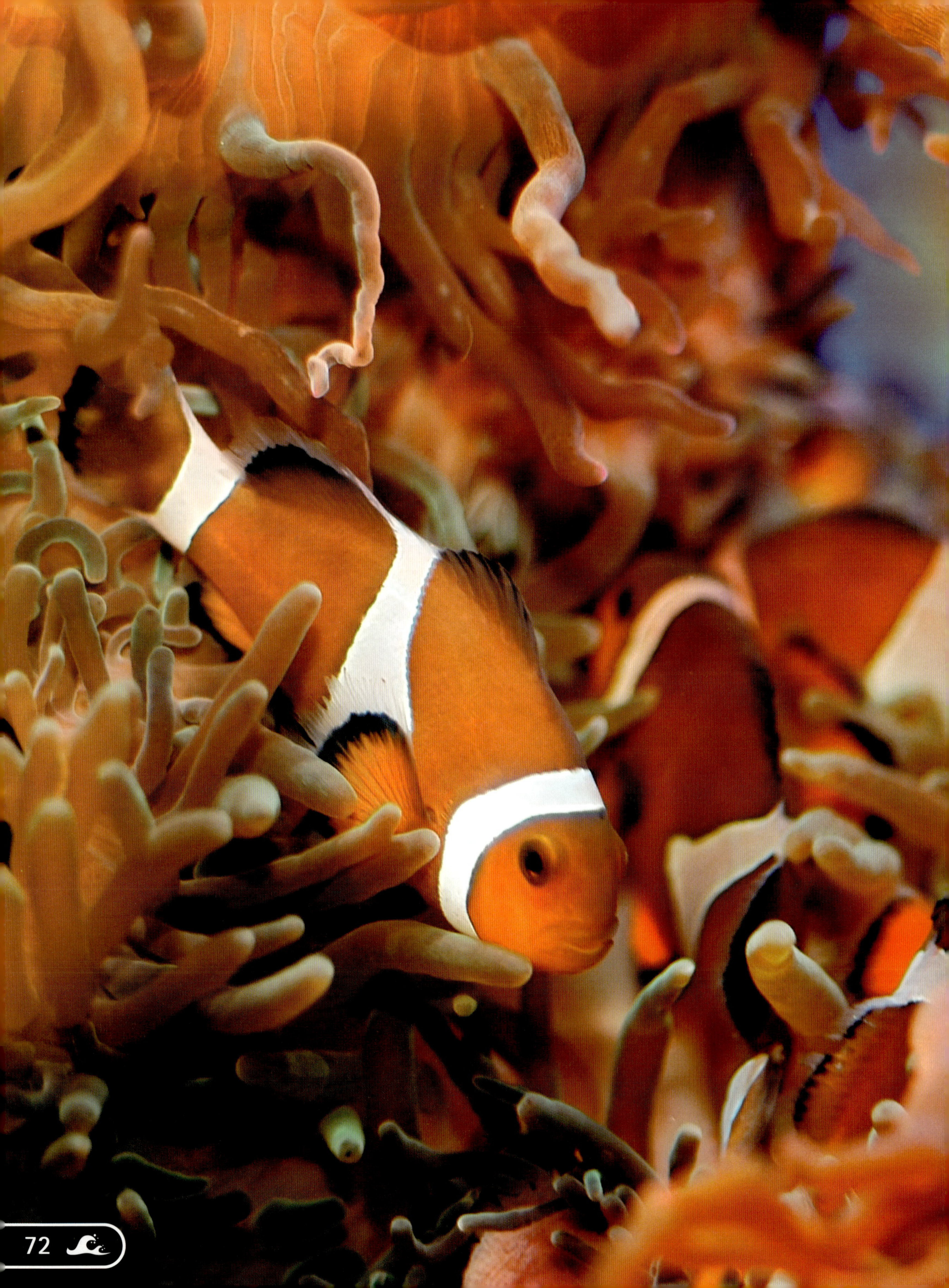

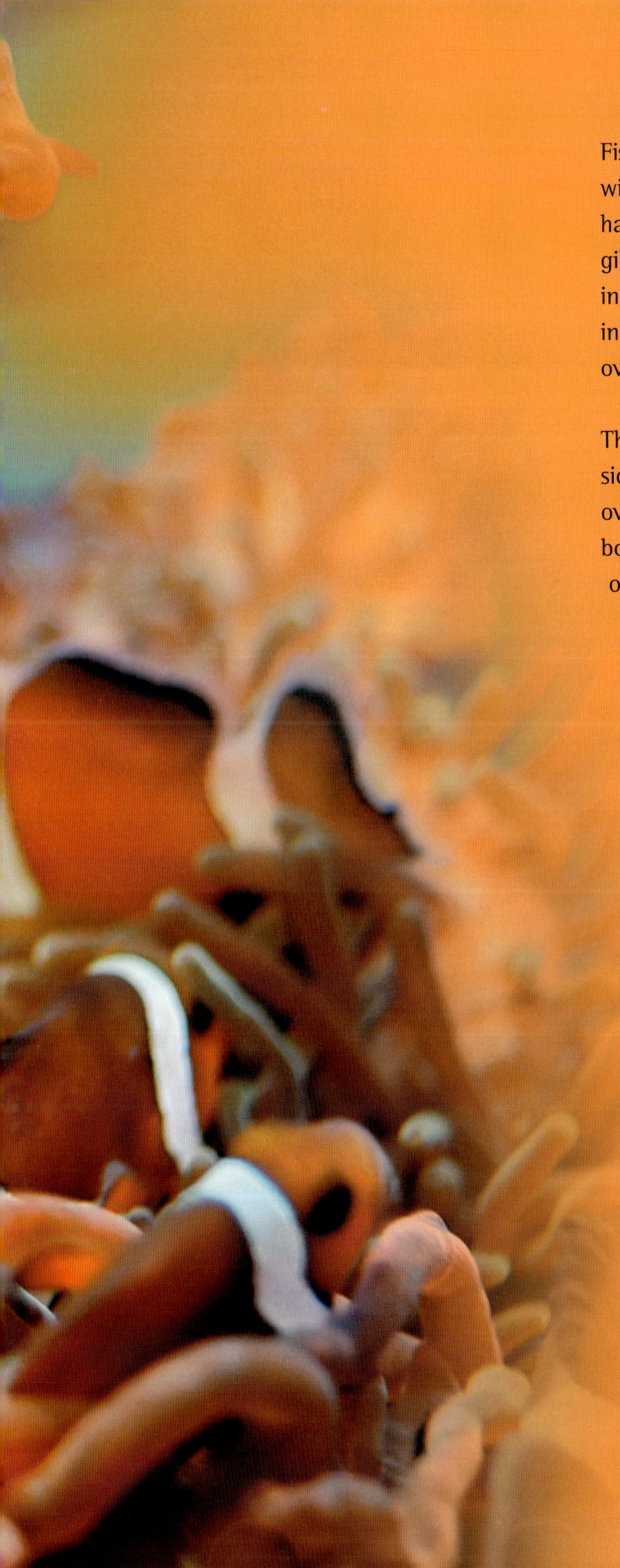

Fish

Fish are cold-blooded aquatic vertebrates (animals with backbones). Some have bony skeletons, others have skeletons made of cartilage, all breathe with gills, but some also breathe with lungs, some live in fresh water like lakes and rivers, others live only in salt water. All fish lay eggs – but some are ovoviviparous, and give birth to live young.

The typical fish shape is a body flattened at the sides with a tail, fins, gills and a skin covered in overlapping scales. Other fish are flattened top to bottom, like flounders, and other such fish that live on the bottom of the sea.

Others, like the tuna, are more streamlined for speed, while still others have tube-shaped, snake-like bodies, like eels or hagfish, which allow them to wriggle into less accessible places in search of food.

A fish's smooth scales grow from the skin and, along with the secretion of oils or slime help make the fish slippery so it can move through the water more easily.

Jawless fish

Lampreys and hagfish have long bodies that look like a snake or an eel, round mouths and small eyes, or none at all. As they have no jaws, they are unable to chew, so suck their food instead. Lamprey and hagfish have rounded gills unlike the longer gills of most fish – they look a little bit like the portholes of a ship or submarine. Also, unlike other fish, they do not have scales but rather a slimy or smooth skin.

▼ How does a hagfish defend itself?

Hagfish are the most primitive of all the fishes and are pretty unpleasant creatures. They can produce large volumes of thick slime from mucus sacs when caught. This distracts the predator and helps the hagfish escape. Once clear, they will tie themselves in a knot, which moves all the way down their body from the head to tail and scrapes off the mucus. Hagfish are scavengers, eating dead or injured fish, or attacking those caught in fishing nets.

▶ Where do you find hagfish?

Hagfish live near the mouth of rivers and spend much of their time buried in mud, with their barbels (which are a bit like fleshy whiskers) and snout sticking out, waiting for their next meal. Some live deep down on the ocean floor and one, Eptatretus strickrotti, was even found near a hydrothermal vent. It was only discovered in 2005, showing how much we still have to learn about the world's oceans. Hagfish depend on their sense of smell to find their food.

Scientists think that the hagfish's nearly identical ancestors were around more than 550 million years ago.

A hagfish may also use its slime to defend its meal from other species and to protect its eggs.

74

▶ What do lampreys eat?

Most adult lampreys feed by attaching themselves to the sides of other fish, and rasping a hole in their skin with their mouths using toothed, sandpaper-like tongues. Once the hole is made, they start sucking out the blood and other body fluids of their victims. They can produce 'anticoagulants' with their saliva. These are substances that stop the blood of their host from clotting and forming a scab to heal.

Lampreys don't have jaws, but their mouths are full of rows of sharp teeth that rasp the flesh of their victims.

How long is a lamprey? Sea lampreys can reach between 1 and 3 feet/30 to 90 centimeters in length.

Boiled lampreys used to be a delicacy. In 1135, King Henry I of England died in Normandy after gorging himself on them!

Where do lampreys live?

Lampreys live in both fresh and salt water worldwide, usually migrating from salt water to fresh to spawn. Some are pretty tough: the arctic lamprey manages to survive in the colder waters around Alaska and sometimes even further north. Some species live in land-locked areas, meaning they do not have access to the sea. Not all lampreys are parasites on fish, however – some, like the European brook lamprey, feed on algae and small organic matter.

Rays and skates

Rays and skates are cartilaginous fish – this means their skeletons, like those of sharks, are made out of a tough, rubbery material called cartilage, instead of bone. Many of the approximately 300 species of rays and skates live near the seabed, but some patrol nearer the surface. They have large wings on each side of their bodies, which they flap like a bird's wings to move along. Their gill openings are behind their eyes on the top sides of their bodies, with their gills positioned on their undersides.

Most manta rays have a wingspan of about 14 feet/4 meters but some as large as 26 feet 3 inches/8 meters have been recorded.

▼ Are sting rays dangerous?

They can be, with their long, spiny whipping tails. Normally they are not aggressive animals and they are unlikely to attack humans unless threatened. If they are pestered, caught or stepped on, however, then their tails can whip out and sting with a poison that that flows from the grooves in the side of their tail spikes. The rough tail stingray is one of the largest and it can reach up to 14 feet/4.3 meters from front to tail tip and could deliver a nasty wound.

▲ Why do manta rays leap out of the water?

Manta rays are thought to leap out of the water to rid themselves of parasites, or to stun small fish by crashing down on top of them. It may be to escape predators or part of a courtship display. It could even be simply because they enjoy it. It is certainly spectacular: sometimes they even perform a full somersault. They are not dangerous animals, unless harpooned, when their thrashing, powerful bodies can be quite destructive. Mantas usually travel alone, but have been observed swimming in pairs, or in groups of up to six individuals.

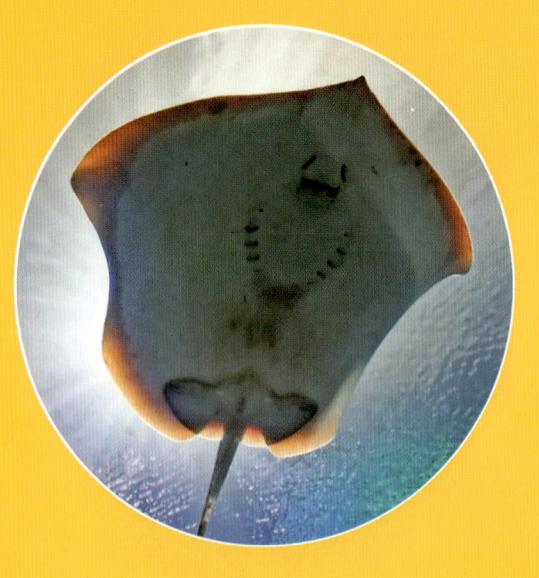

Most stingrays eat worms, crustaceans or mollusks, but some attack larger fish.

What is an electric ray's shock for?

Electric rays are often quite slow moving, so their electrical charge can be used to stun quicker prey. It also serves as protection against predators – the shock would be enough to frighten away many, and is strong enough to stun a human. However, electric rays mainly eat worms, crustaceans and other small animals that are slow moving, so it is thought that they may also use their electrical charge to help navigate or tell each other apart.

Torpedo rays can generate 170 to 220 volts – nearly as much as the plug socket in a house.

What is a mermaid's purse?

Like many rays, skates and sharks, the New Zealand rough skate lays an egg case that has coiled tendrils at each of its corners with which it can be anchored to rocks or plants at the bottom of the sea. The young take several months to hatch, and are vulnerable to predators during this time. When these egg cases wash up on the beach, they are known as a mermaid's purse.

How much does a manta ray weigh? The heaviest ever recorded was 3,100lbs/1,400kg.

The New Zealand rough skate grows to a length of about 3 feet/1 meter.

Sharks

Like other cartilaginous fish, sharks have a rough skin, and they cannot fold their fins. Sharks have strong jaws and many have sharp, teeth, but some have flat grinding teeth. Sharks have a highly developed sense of smell and can sniff out food from huge distances. There are around 350 species of shark, which includes some of the largest fish in the world.

Which is the fastest shark?

It is thought that the short-finned Mako shark is the fastest. This shark is well-adapted for speed and energy-efficiency. It is very streamlined and agile. It may manage bursts of speed up to 70 miles/110 kilometers per hour but these estimates are thought to be a little high. Others put its top-speed at something closer to around 50 miles/80 kilometers per hour. It eats other fish such as tuna, which are also some of the fastest swimming fish.

How do great whites locate their prey?

At close range, the great white can detect the electrical currents generated by another animal's body. When further away, it has a powerful sense of smell that can track the scent of fish from a great distance. Great whites have good eyesight, with well-developed irises that can respond to light. They can see well in the dark and have a good sense of hearing.

The maximum known length of a great white is at least 20 feet/6 meters, but individuals as large as 23 feet/7 meters are thought possible.

▶ **What is the world's largest fish?**

It's the whale shark, which lives in tropical and subtropical waters, often close to the coast. It feeds by swimming just below the surface with its huge mouth held open, gathering plankton that it can filter from the water with specially adapted gills. It sometimes eats assorted small fish, sardines, and even fish as large as mackerel can get swallowed up along the way.

Whale sharks can grow over 50 feet/14 meters in length, and can weigh up to 12 tons.

How many people are killed by sharks? Shark attacks on humans are rare, and only between 6 and 10 people each year are killed in attacks.

▶ **Why do hammerhead sharks have such weird heads?**

There is a lot of debate about why this might be. Some think it is to help with hydrodynamics (movement through the water) and point out how similar it is to the front of a Formula One race car. They seem to be able to move them the outsides of their hammerheads, which might help them stay buoyant as they move through the water. Other biologists think it is to help their sense of smell – most hammerheads have nostrils on the outermost tips of their heads with special grooves to channel water over them.

Hammerheads grow up to 13 feet/4 meters long and are found in warm seas.

Coelacanths, lungfish and arapaima

Coelacanths and lungfish belong to the order 'sarcopterigii'. They are bony fish with pairs of rounded, fleshy fins resembling what some scientist expect to be the likely form of the limbs of early land-dwelling animals. Lungfish and arapaima can also breathe air with a basic type of lung when their environment dries up. Although lungfish and arapaima are unrelated, both animals live in freshwater.

What is a coelacanth?

Coelacanths are by far the oldest vertebrates alive today. They were thought to be extinct until one was discovered in a fishing net in the late 1930s. Coelacanths have large scales and can weigh as much as 160lbs/72kg. Their most distinctive feature is their fins, which are lobes supported by their skeletons with an elaborate system of muscles allowing them to move in a variety of positions.

How old are Coelacanth? They first appear in fossil records over 400 million years ago.

◀ What are some African lungfish famous for?

There are four species of African lungfish famous for the mud cocoons they build to protect themselves when the lake or river in which they live dries up. They dig holes in the mud then cover themselves completely with a secretion of mucus from their bodies. As the water level lowers, these secretions dry to form a leathery cocoon that encases the fish until sufficient water has returned. During this time they use their lungs to breathe air through tube-like vents and their metabolic rate slows down.

African lungfish have longer, cord-like fins, rather than the more fleshy limbs of the Australian variety.

▲ How are Australian lungfish different to other lungfish?

Australian lungfish are the most primitive of the lungfishes. They have only one lung, unlike the South American or African lungfish which have two. Unlike other lungfish, the waters in which the Australian lungfish live do not dry up completely each year, so they do not have to form a 'cocoon' or burrow of mud to protect themselves from drying out. Instead, the Australian lungfish uses its lung when the water it lives in becomes stagnant or polluted.

What is an arapaima?

An arapaima is another type of fish that can breathe air as well as in water. It is also the largest fish to spend all of its time in fresh water. Arapaimas live in warm rivers and swamps in South America where they eat snakes, fish, frogs, insects and sometimes turtles. The lakes and rivers in which they live are often so warm and slow-flowing that there isn't enough oxygen, so the fish swim to the surface to gulp fresh air.

The female arapaima lays eggs in a nest it fans clear of debris at the bottom of its water habitat.

Schooling fish

Many species of fish form large populations and migrate around the oceans. These large movements of fish, swimming together almost as one, are some of the most spectacular sights in nature. The reasons for this behavior are many and complex. There are a number of theories that suggest that forming schools can improve a species' chances in a number of different ways, be they reproductive, energy saving, food gathering or protection.

▼ Why do herring form schools?

Herring move in huge schools of slow moving individuals for the long trip to their spawning grounds in the Baltic Sea. On their way, however, they feed on tiny crustaceans that are very nimble swimmers that can sense the approach of a fish and make fast evasive manoeuvres. Faced with a mass of thousands of individuals, however, it is impossible for these crustaceans to get out of the way of all of them. In this way, by moving in large schools, fish such as herring increase their chances of catching food that would be much more difficult to catch on their own.

▼ How do fish choose their school?

Many fish seem to choose to join larger schools of fish that are similar in size or age or coloring. This probably lowers their chances of being eaten because it may confuse predators: predatory fish have been seen picking off those fish that 'stand out'. Interestingly, experiments with color choice have shown that these decisions are based on a type of 'imprinting'. This means that it could be a learned behavior, rather than genetic.

A school of herring can contain millions of individuals, all of them roughly the same size.

Tuna live in warm and temperate seas around the world.

What is a frigate mackerel?

Frigate mackerels are another type of fish, related to the tuna, which swim around in large numbers. They move in groups and are often seen in one area and then not seen again for years, like the ship, called a frigate, that used to roam the seas in ages past. As they swim around the oceans, they are prey to a number of species of large hunting fish, so large groups improve the chances of an individual not getting eaten. Living in schools also improves the chances of finding a mate and reproducing.

How fast can a tuna swim?

Tuna often cruise at about 30 miles/50 kilometers per hour. Tuna have one of the most streamlined bodies of all fish and they are also one of the fastest swimmers, and cover vast distances. They must always keep moving, though, to keep a steady supply of oxygen over their gills. One reason they may form schools is to preserve energy: one fish will use the pressure field, or slipstream, formed behind another as they cut through the water.

What is the top speed of a tuna?

About 40 miles/64 kilometers per hour.

Migrating fish

Many species of fish migrate in different ways and for various reasons. There are several types of migration. 'Diadromous' fish travel between salt and fresh water and these can be split into 'anadromous' fish, such as salmon, that live most of their lives in the sea but return to fresh water to spawn and 'catadromous' fish, like freshwater eels, that live mainly in fresh water and breed in the sea. Other fish migrate around the oceans and seas.

▼ What is diel vertical migration?

Like many fish, lantern fish make 'diel vertical' (or 'daily vertical') migrations every day. At night they migrate towards the surface, then retreat back down to the darker depths during daytime. It is thought that they do this to avoid predators and to follow the movements of zooplankton. The lantern fish takes its name from the lights on its body. Each species has a different pattern of lights to aid recognition in the depths of the ocean.

A female eel, if 'land-locked' in a lake with no access to the sea, can live for 50 years, without spawning.

The lights on lantern fish can be pale green, blue and sometimes even yellow or red.

Where do freshwater eels spawn?

The European and American freshwater eels both spawn in the same area of the Atlantic Ocean, called the Sargasso Sea. At this time, a female eel can lay as many as 10 to 20 million eggs. After spawning, the adults die and the baby eels swim and drift in the ocean. European eels then make a journey of 3,000 miles/4,800 kilometers back to rivers across Europe.

▶ Do Atlantic salmon die after spawning?

Unlike many species of salmon, Atlantic salmon can manage more than one spawning. They are born in rivers, where they eat small animals like bugs, then swim out to sea, gathering in large feeding areas to grow into adults. This takes two to four years. Once they are mature, they make the long trip back to the same river in which they hatched using a keen sense of smell. These 'runs' occur in the fall.

The Atlantic salmon can make leaps 12 feet/3.7 meters high and over 16 feet/5 meters long!

How many species of lantern fish are there? Over 150.

▼ How do sea trout migrate?

Sea trout, like Atlantic salmon, hatch from eggs deposited in fresh water. The young have yolk sacs attached with a month's supply of food inside. After about three years of living in the river, sea trout develop changes in its gills to enable it to cope with salt water. Its first migration usually takes place early in summer, and once at sea it feeds quickly. It can spend up to another three years at sea, before returning to the river for the first time.

Sea trout can live up to about 20 years (but most live for a much shorter period) during which time they may return to spawn on a number of occasions.

Deep sea fish

The deep sea represents 80 percent of the total area inhabited by living things. As the sea gets deeper, it gets darker. At a depth of about 500 feet/150 meters, there is little if any light left and colors are no longer visible to the human eye. It also gets colder, making life harder and, to human eyes, less familiar. Creatures that live in the deepest reaches cannot survive the pressure change if brought to the surface.

▼ What is the most common deep-sea fish?

By far the most common type of deep sea fish are the rattails, so-called because of their slender bodies, which taper to a thin tail. Scientists have discovered that this type of fish has particularly high levels of the chemical urea in their bodies, which then helps maintain hydration levels while living in concentrated salt water. Without the urea, water would move from areas of low salinity (the fish's body) to areas of high salinity (the surrounding ocean water), and the fish would become dehydrated by the surrounding ocean water.

Giant rattail fish can be larger than 3 feet /1 meter long.

What is a fangtooth?

Fangtooth is another bizarre and ugly fish from the deep. Although it looks fierce, it only grows to about 6 inches/7.5 centimeters long. It has a short, deep body with a large head and mouth and is covered with prickly scales. As its name suggests, it has very long and pointed teeth – those in the lower jaw slide into pockets in the roof of the mouth when the jaws close. Deep in the ocean, food is scarce, so the fangtooth eats just about anything it can find!

The color of the adult fangtooth ranges from dark brown to black. Juveniles are light gray in color, with long spines on their heads.

By day, viperfish live at depth of over 8,200 feet/ 2,500 meters. They rise to about 1,500 feet/ 450 meters at night.

▲ Is the viperfish as nasty as it looks and sounds?

Viperfish are easily recognized by their long body and sharp, fanged teeth – so long that they don't even fit in its mouth and instead project back close to its eyes. It is thought that they may use these to impale their victims when swimming at high speeds, as its first vertebra, just behind the head, acts as a shock absorber. The fish is also thought to sometimes swim at 45 degrees, sticking out its sharp teeth. Viperfish have bioluminescent lights along their sides, which possibly lure prey towards them.

What makes the angler fish's light? It is made by millions of luminescent bacteria.

▶ How does an angler fish hunt?

The deep-sea angler fish uses a fishing pole-like projection on the top of its head that has developed from the first spine in its front dorsal fin. Sensing the presence of prey nearby, the anglerfish begins fishing with the top of this pole flickering and shimmering in the black water around it. As its prey is lured in, it brings the pole closer to its vast, fanged mouth then drops its lower jaw and expands its gill covers, swallowing it. Apart from its, sometimes luminous, angling tips, the angler fish is generally dark brown or black in color.

Male deep sea anglers start as free swimming fish, with large eyes, but no rod or lure and no digestive tube.

Bottom dwellers

Bottom-dwelling fish spend their time feeding on the bottom of the ocean, in deep or shallow water. Many bury themselves or have flattened or camouflaged bodies and their heads, mouths and eyes may be strangely arranged to suit their different lifestyles. Some bottom dwellers feed off small organisms or plants, or the detritus of the ocean floor, but there are also plenty of ready to feed on any other bottom dwellers they find.

▼ Why do stonefish just lie around?

Lying still on the bottom of the sea is one of the best ways of conserving energy and many bottom-dwelling fish, like the stonefish, are very good at this. Most have developed camouflage as a protection, as otherwise they might be easy prey. The stonefish, however, goes one step further for protection and has extremely potent venom glands at the base of its strong spines. These are so sharp that they can even puncture the rubber sole of a shoe.

Stonefish venom is fast-acting and is potentially fatal to humans.

▼ Do stargazers really gaze at stars?

Not really, but they look like they do. Their eyes and mouths are both on the tops of their heads, which makes them look like they are gazing upwards. They are quite chunky-bodied and look a bit like toads. Like many bottom-dwelling fish, they bury themselves with only their eyes and mouths showing, some with a worm-like thread in their mouths with which to lure small fishes.

Stargazers can generate an electrical charge with special organs behind their eyes developed from the optic nerve.

▶ Are there any bottom-dwelling sharks?

Many types of fish have bottom-dwelling counterparts. A shark called the monkfish, or angel shark, spends its life searching through the sandy bottom of the sea at depths of up to 330 feet/100 meters. Like many other bottom dwellers, it has a flat body and camouflaging coloring or markings – in this case brown, gry, or creamy yellowish skin with brown and blue spots. Monkfish eat small seabed fish and detect prey using their electro-senses.

Monkfish often partially bury themselves in sand.

How strong is the stargazer's electric shock? About 50 volts.

The peacock flounder's body can change to a lighter or darker shade, depending on its surroundings.

Why are flounders flat?

When flounders first hatch, they look like most other fishes swimming in the water, but, before long, they start to lean to one side. Then the eye on the underside starts to move, until both eyes are on the 'top'. As the eye moves, the skull also twists round, with the mouth often ending up on top also. What is now the underside of the fish, then starts to lose its pigment and becomes white, as the topside darkens to blend in with the surrounding area.

Coral reef fish

Coral reefs are formed by the skeletons of corals – these reef-building corals live in colonies and bind together to form large structures. A coral reef is a thriving community for many species and all have their preferred niches – some like the shallower zones, others prefer the shelter of deeper regions. It is a very complex system of inter-dependent relationships containing an amazing diversity of life.

▼ What is the biggest fish on the coral reef?

Giant groupers are the biggest bony fish that normally live on coral reefs. They can weigh as much as 660-880lbs/300-400kg – that's heavier than five men. Giant groupers eat lobsters, other fish and even small sharks, and often live in deep holes or caves. Because of their size, they are not very fearful of attack and are generally slow-moving when not hunting. Their mouths are wide and their markings often blend with their surroundings.

Giant groupers can live for up to 40 years.

◄ Why do clownfish live in sea anemones?

Clownfish are a type of anemone fish that are often spotted in small groups living around sea anemones. Clownfish are immune to the venom in the sea anemones' stinging tentacles, so gain protection from larger predators. In return for this protection, clownfish clear the anemone of debris and chase away butterfly fish, which eat its tentacles.

Clownfish are quite bold for their size and will chase away much larger fish, especially when guarding eggs.

▶ How do queen angelfish defend themselves?

The queen angelfish is probably one of the prettiest fish on the coral reef and has some interesting markings. It is named 'queen' because of a spot on the top of its head, that some think looks a bit like a crown. It also has a spot on its front fins and mouth. These spots are like false eyes, and confuse predators over the fish's direction of movement, size and the possible location of vital areas such as the head, eyes and gills.

Most angelfish are solitary and swim constantly, often on a set route.

Why are lionfish striped?

Lionfish are also known as scorpionfish, and are often quite boldly colored. As elsewhere in nature, these bright stripes of color may warn of potential danger to attackers. However, when on a crowded and colorful coral reef, it is surprising how well its typical red, brown and white bands blend in with its surroundings. Some species have grooved venom spines located on their head and in their fins, and the stings can cause severe pain to humans.

Why do clownfish not get stung?

Their bodies are protected by a coating of mucus.

A lionfish's spines act like hypodermic needles, injecting poison from glands at their base.

Freshwater fish

Freshwater fish live in streams, rivers, lakes or canals rather than the open sea. Freshwater only makes up about two to three percent of all the world's water (mostly in the polar ice caps, and less the one percent of the Earth's surface, and yet it contains a huge variety of species. These habitats are at risk due to human activity and pollution.

Species of Siamese fighting fish have been selectively bred as pets – some even have fins longer than their bodies.

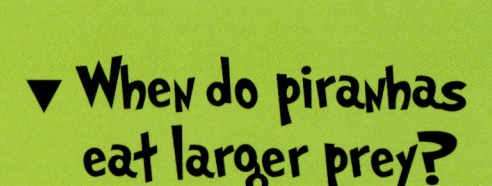

▼ How do jewel cichlids care for their young?

The jewel cichlid is normally a quarrelsome, aggressive fish that is very territorial. However, these animals mate for life and have a highly developed sense of brood care, giving their young a better chance of survival. After the eggs have been laid and fertilized, the adult pair guard the nest. One will fan water over the eggs, while the other stands guard. Even as young fish, the parents continue to care for them, protecting them from predators.

▼ When do piranhas eat larger prey?

Red piranhas are perhaps one of the most famous carnivorous freshwater fish. Usually, these predators feed on other, smaller fishes, but they can also eat much larger prey. This is usually only as a result of a chance encounter with a wounded animal. A sudden strong smell of blood can send piranhas into a frenzy searching for the source. When they find it, a large school of piranhas can strip a pig-sized animal to bare bones within minutes. Each fish makes repeated, lightening strikes with its razor-sharp teeth.

Piranhas are mainly found in South America, where locals have used their sharp teeth as weapons.

Normally a slightly duller color, jewel cichlids change to bright red at mating time.

How do Siamese fighting fish fight?

The dramatically colored and large finned male Siamese fighting fish are very territorial and will fight bitterly if one invades the other's space. To start with, they spread out their fins in a display of aggression to deter rivals. If this doesn't work, they will then lunge for each other, biting and tearing at the others' fins. Eventually, one will give up and leave.

What is the largest freshwater fish? The Mekong giant catfish.

The pike is Britain's largest freshwater fish and can reach 6 feet/1.8 meters in length.

▶ How do pikes hunt?

Like many carnivorous fish, the pike is an ambush predator that lies in wait for its prey and then strikes suddenly. Pikes are solitary predators that hide in reeds or behind rocks. When prey approaches, the fish rushes out, aided by its slim, streamlined, elongated body. Larger pike have even been known to hunt ducklings and young coots from the surface of lakes. They have strong, beak-like jaws and sharp teeth.

93

Eels and catfish

Catfish are characterized by their whisker-like sensory barbles on their upper and lower jaws. Their heads and mouths are broad and they have quite small eyes. Many species also have strong, sharp-pointed spines in their dorsal and pectoral fins. There are 20 families of eels, and all have long, thin bodies and spineless fins. In most, their fins form one long continuous fin over the rear of the body and their skin is covered with small scales.

▼ What is different about conger eels?

Conger eels are different from morays because of their pectoral fins and the black margins on its top and bottom fins. Prior to spawning, the female conger eel's body changes. She stops feeding and starts using a large amount of her energy to produce eggs. Conger eels migrate from the Black sea or Iceland to the spawning grounds between the Azores and Gibraltar, where the female then lays between three and eight million eggs in deep water.

The conga eel is mature at an age of five to 15 years, and spawns in summer.

How does a moray eel catch its prey?

Typically a moray eel, such as a green moray, will anchor the rear portion of its body into rocks or a coral reef and allow the front of its body to move with the sea. It holds this position with its mouth gaped, ready to strike at any prey that comes close. Morays are usually nocturnal, but will sometimes leave their lairs during the day if food is available.

The green moray eel usually grows to about 5 feet/1.5 meters in length, but can be up to 10 feet/3 meters long.

The talking catfish can reach a length of about 8 inches/ 20 centimeters.

▶ How do talking catfish talk?

The 'talking catfish' is so called because it makes a croaking sound, especially when caught. These grunts are caused by vibrating their 'air bladders' and by the movement of its pectoral fins. Although it is from a different group, talking catfish are also called 'armored catfish' because of a row of thick, overlapping spiny plates along each side of their body. Their spiny fins can inflict painful stabs that take a long time to heal, so they are armed as well as armored.

▼ Can armored catfish survive out of water?

Armored catfish have a special air bladder contained within a bony casing and separated into two parts. They gulp air at the surface of the water, which they store in the air bladder. In armored catfish, the air bladder works like a simple lung and oxygen is absorbed into the fish's bloodstream. These catfish can survive for long periods out of water, especially if they are kept moist.

Some armored catfish build nests from plants and bubbles formed with saliva to protect their eggs.

How many eggs does the armored catfish lay? Up to 200 at one time.

Flying fish, seahorses, pipefish and sea dragons

All species of seahorse are marine, whereas some species of pipefish can live in freshwater. Both have very small scales that form into rings of hard, protective armor. They have long, fluted snouts for sucking in tiny animals and algae from the water and have long tails with which they can hold onto things. Atlantic flying fish are strong swimmers, reaching high speeds. Their fins are 'soft-rayed' or spineless.

Seahorses, pipefish and sea dragons can move their eyes independently, like chameleons.

How are pipefish different to seahorses?

Pipefish are identical to seahorses apart from how their bodies are arranged. As their name suggests, their bodies are stretched out in a long pipe shape. Many pipefish live in and around corals and are well-camouflaged, sometimes spectacularly so, like the harlequin ghost pipefish. Ghost pipefish brood their eggs in their enlarged pelvic fins. Some pipefish prefer shallow water, and can be found in rock pools at low tide.

Which is the largest seahorse?

The largest seahorse is the Pacific seahorse, which can reach a length of 1 foot/30 centimeters. Like all seahorses, they swim very slowly by rippling their dorsal fin behind them and guiding themselves with their pectorals, taking rests by holding onto seaweeds with their tails. They have larger than usual air bladders to help them float because their shape is not very buoyant. Seahorses are abundant in shallow, subtropical and tropical seas.

Most species of seahorse mate for life and have been seen giving each other greeting displays each morning.

▶ What do leafy sea dragons look like?

Leafy sea dragons are some of the best camouflaged animals in the world. They are almost impossible to see among the seaweeds and sea grasses in which they hide, with elaborate leafy flaps that look exactly like leafy growths attached all over their bodies. These flaps are solely for disguise purposes. Sea dragons do not have tails that can grip on to things, and live in shallow water off the coast of Australia.

Female sea dragons lay their eggs on the male's tail, where they grow until they hatch.

How long can a flying fish stay in the air? As long as 30 seconds!

How do flying fish fly?

The Atlantic flying fish manages its flight by reaching a top speed of as much as 40 miles/65 kilometers per hour, vibrating its tail fin at up to 50 times a second. It then shoots up to the surface, breaking through into the air. It extends its large pectoral fins and holds them stiffly, gliding. At the same time they vibrate their lower tail to help keep momentum. It is thought that they do this in order to escape predators, rather than to catch food.

A flying fish can sometimes glide for over 330 feet/100 meters, but most flights are for about 130 feet/40 meters.

Hunting fish

Blue marlin and sailfish are known as 'billfish' because of their large bills, which are long and rounded. The swordfish is slightly different and has a longer, flatter bill, and so is grouped separately. All three of these fish are very muscular and fast, and the marlin and sailfish are known to leap out of the water. The barracuda is another, unrelated, hunting fish and has an elongated body and strong jaws with sharp, fang-like teeth. All these fish are found in tropical and subtropical oceans.

Barracudas have forked tails, large eyes and dark blotches on a background of silvery scales.

▶ How do marlins swim?

Like the swordfish and sailfish, marlin have two ways of swimming that use two different sets of muscle – one fast and one slow. One is for when they are cruising and conserving energy on longer trips and the other is for shorter bursts of high speed, which can be up to 50 miles/ 80 kilometers an hour. Although not usually dangerous to humans, marlins have sometimes leapt out of the water and speared unlucky fishermen trying to catch them.

Because they are so fast and strong, the blue marlin and sailfish are prized catches for human fishermen.

How do barracudas hunt?

Barracudas are curious animals that are attracted mainly to shiny, flashing objects that look like fish scales. It is therefore thought that they hunt using sight more than smell. Barracudas are often solitary, ambush predators but younger fish congregate in shoals and can hunt in packs. They eat all kinds of smaller fish and sometimes herd shoals of them together when they are full, waiting until they are hungry enough for another meal.

▼ How fast is a sailfish?

Sailfish are the fastest fish in the sea, reaching speeds of nearly 70 miles/110 kilometers an hour, although more usually swimming at speeds of 60 miles/96 kilometers an hour. Sailfish have extremely streamlined bodies and huge sail fins which are folded back when swimming, but raised when it feels threatened. They reach lengths of 12 feet/ 3.6 meters and their bodies are packed tight with muscles. They can swipe their tails quickly to generate bursts of speed and they have been known to injure sharks, although this is thought to be accidental while chasing the same food.

▼ How is a swordfish different from a marlin?

Swordfish have longer bills or 'swords' than the marlin – it can account for up to 30 percent of their overall body length – and are slightly larger overall. They also lose their teeth and scales as they grow older and they lack the longer, strap-like ventral fins of the sailfish or marlin. They hunt using their bills to slash at, injure and stun their food, which they then swallow. Swordfish can weigh as much as 1,200lbs/550kg.

A swordfish's sword is made of bone covered by tough skin.

Sailfish eat fish and squid, chasing them at high speeds through the water.

How long can swordfish live? More than 25 years.

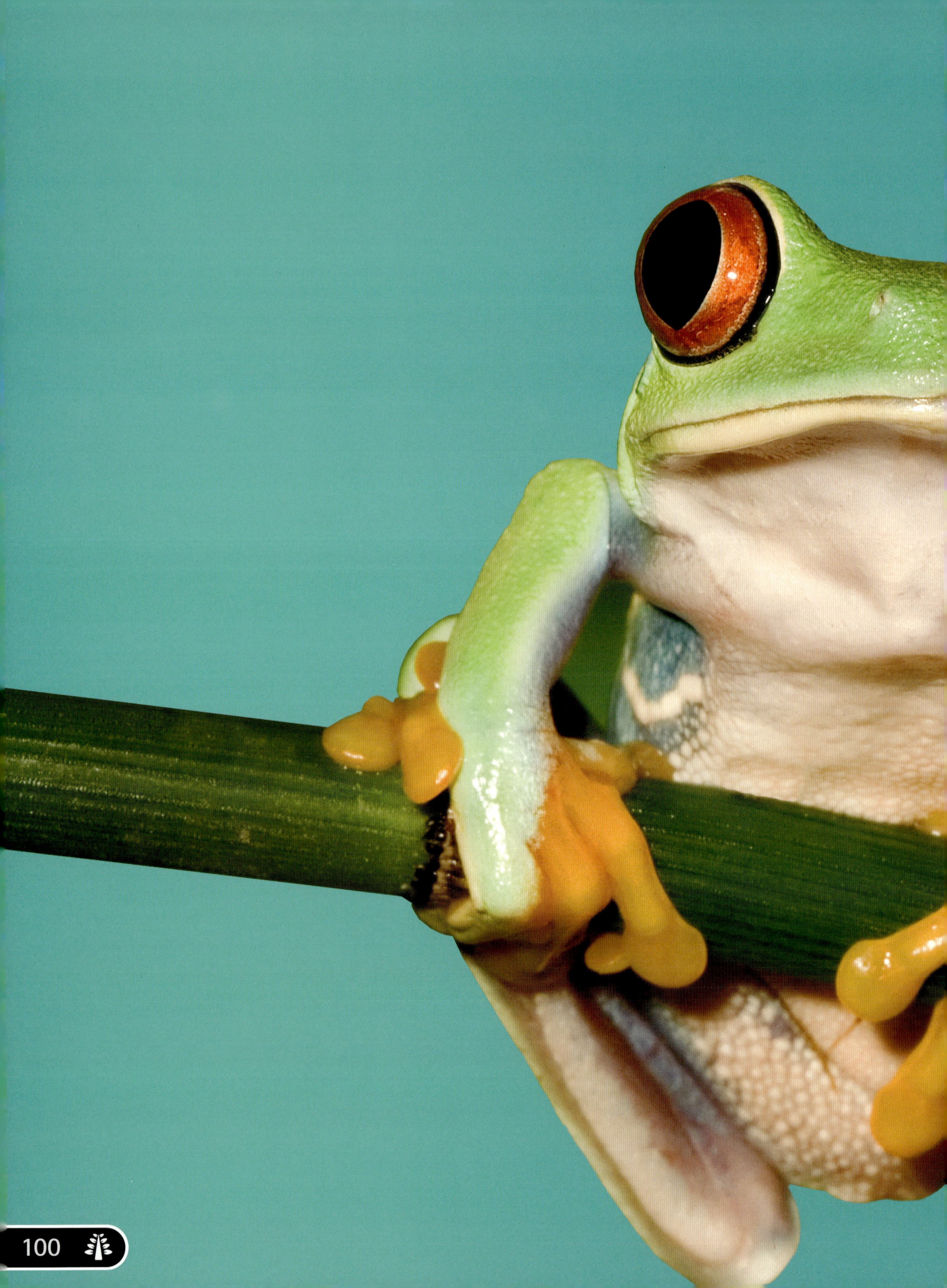

Amphibians

Amphibians spend their lives on land as well as in water. All adult amphibians are predators, living by feeding on other animals. Their skin is permeable, thin and moist, and doesn't have a protective coating like other vertebrates – feathers on birds, scales on fish or reptiles, or hair on mammals.

Amphibians keep their skin moist with a type of mucus secreted from a number of glands. Often these secretions can be toxic, either to deter predators or to keep them clean in order to prevent infection. Their skin can be smooth or warty and is often brightly colored or patterned. All amphibians can also breathe through their skin.

Most adult amphibians have webbed feet, to help them swim, and most have large, protruding eyes, to help with night vision, as many are nocturnal. They have rounded or narrowed pupils. Rounded and horizontally narrowed pupils are suited to the daytime, while vertically narrowed pupils help with night vision.

Many amphibians' life cycles go through three distinct phases: females lay eggs, which hatch into larvae, which then change shape into adults. This process is called metamorphosis.

Newts and salamanders

Newts and salamanders are amphibians that look like lizards, but they do not have scales. They are usually active at night and they have long, slender bodies and quite short limbs, but with long tails. In total, there are over 450 species but this is likely to increase as more continue to be found. Some species can climb trees, but most hide under rocks or logs until darkness or wet weather arrives. They often lay their eggs in water, but many salamanders lay their eggs on land.

Female fire salamanders lay larvae in streams, rather than eggs like other newts and salamanders.

▼ How do Japanese fire-bellied newts swim?

Japanese fire-bellied newts use their long, flattened slender tails by wriggling them from side to side. It is a species that spends most of its life in water and is a fast and agile swimmer. Like many newts and salamanders, its bright coloring warns that it can produce toxins that are harmful or that taste unpleasant. Mating pairs go through a long courtship of water dances during which the male fans and beats his tail rapidly at the female.

▲ How do fire salamanders protect themselves?

Fire salamanders have two rows of enlarged glands, called parotid glands, running along the middle of their backs from which they are able to spray toxic secretions. They can direct these sprays quite accurately over distances of nearly 6.5 feet/2 meters. These toxins can affect the central nervous systems of their predators and cause eyes and mouths to itch. After their larval stage, fire salamanders spend nearly all their lives on land.

Japanese fire-bellied newts are often active during the day.

How much time does an adult newt spend in the water? Anywhere between one and 210 days a year.

🌱 Olms can reach a length of 1 foot/30 centimeters.

🌱 The red-bellied newt contains enough toxins to kill a man, so it warns predators not to eat it.

▲ What is an olm?

An olm is a species of salamander that never really seems to grow up! Instead, they keep many of their larval features for life. Adult salamanders can breathe through their skin and can also breathe through lungs. The olms, however, keep the gills that salamanders have as larvae and never shed them. They are also faded in color, often in washed out grays, pinks or yellows. They have very small eyes but large tails to help them swim.

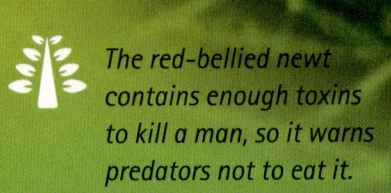

Why does the red-bellied newt curl itself into a circle?

When the red-bellied newt curls itself up it is performing an unusual behavior pattern known as the 'unken' reflex. This is named after the fire-bellied toad, called 'unke' in German, which also behaves this way. When threatened, the red-bellied newt shuts its eyes, stretches out its legs and bends its head and tail back over its body. This is in order to display as much of the colorful parts of its body as possible. This warns the predator that it tastes bad to eat.

Frogs

Frogs are amphibians with long back legs for jumping. Their anklebones are stretched, which gives them extra leverage when leaping. Frogs differ from toads in that they usually have smooth, shiny skin while toads have duller, warty skin. Frogs are found in humid, hard to reach places such as rainforests, and we have much to discover about them, and new species are still being identified. The most familiar frogs are those that produce spawn in ponds, which hatch into tadpole larvae and then grow into adult frogs.

The nest-building gray frogs live in Southern Africa and, like most frogs, eat insects.

▼ Which is the most poisonous frog?

The golden poison dart frog of South America is the most poisonous frog. It comes in a variety of bright colors – mint green, yellow and orange – each one warning of the nasty surprise it holds for any animal wanting to eat it. It is so poisonous that it is unsafe to handle. The poison dart frogs take their name from the practice of native South American hunters who use the secretions from the skin of these frogs to poison their hunting darts.

▲ Do frogs build nests?

To protect their vulnerable eggs from predators, African gray tree frogs lay their eggs in a foam nest attached to a branch above water. The female produces eggs along with a liquid. Then the male, who holds onto the female during mating, beats this liquid into froth. As the froth hardens, it protects the eggs, creating the nest. A number of different mating pairs may work together on one large, communal nest. These nests are made in trees overhanging water so that when young tadpoles hatch, they drop into the pool.

A dart made from the secretions of a poison dart frog can remain deadly for up to one year.

Which toad looks dead?

The Surinam toad is actually a species of frog that looks as if it has been flattened. As well as being one of the most bizarre-looking of all frogs, it has a strange way of breeding. As the female lays her eggs, the male fertilizes them and places them onto her back, pressing them down with his belly. Over a few days, they sink further into her squidgy skin. In some species, they hatch as tadpoles from her back, but in others they stay embedded until they grow into small frogs!

The Surinam toad finds its food by touch. Its long, slim fingers probe the river bed searching for food.

How many species of frog are there? Over 4,400. More are being found all the time!

▶ Why do Darwin's frogs swallow their young?

They don't but it looks like they do. Female Darwin's frogs lay their eggs on land. Males then gather and wait around eggs that are ready to hatch and gobble up the small tadpoles into their mouths as they emerge. They do not swallow them, however. Instead, the male of one species, Rhinoderma darwinii, hides the tadpoles away in his vocal sac until they are ready to emerge as small frogs! Another similar species, Rhinoderma rufum, carries the tadpoles to water.

Male Darwin's frogs can carry up to 15 tadpoles in their vocal sacs.

Toads

Toads are generally heavier-set than frogs, with shorter legs and more warty-looking skin. They have a large bump behind their eyes known as a parotid gland. Toads are usually ground-dwelling and typically hide in holes during the day, emerging at night to look for food or to mate. Like frogs, they lay eggs that hatch into tadpoles. Many species of toad hunt insects, flicking out their sticky tongues to catch them. Other species ambush their food.

The last emergence of the golden toad was in 1987 and it has not been seen since.

▲ Which are the most colorful toads?

The golden toad lives, or lived, in the rainforests of Costa Rica. They spend most of their lives hidden in holes dug into the extensive root systems of forest trees. They emerge for a few days each year in order to mate in small pools and streams. Male golden toads are a golden orange in color and the females are deep red with large brown blotches – they are one of the most colorful of all toads.

◀ What do cane toads eat?

The cane toad is a very hungry predator indeed. It eats almost anything it can get inside its large mouth including birds, mice and fish, along with the usual insects, slugs and earthworms. Cane toads are native to Texas and South America, but they have been introduced into other areas for pest control. Unfortunately, because of their voracious appetites, such introductions have usually had disastrous results for other local frog or useful insect populations.

The cane toad can grow up to 10 inches/25 centimeters long, and can weigh 2lbs 3 oz/1kg.

▶ Do toads give you warts?

There is no evidence to prove that toads give people warts, but it's not a good idea to pick them up. All toads produce secretions and unpleasant toxins, of varying strengths, to repel predators such as birds, foxes and other animals. Their warts are enlarged skin glands designed to excrete these defenses. A number can be quite dangerous. The Colorado river toad's toxin, for example, can produce powerful hallucinogenic effects in humans if eaten.

Colorado river toads live in the southwestern United States and eat small rodents and insects.

How many eggs can a toad lay? As many as 20,000.

Common toads wait for rainy weather before leaving the pond in which they were born.

Which toad hunts bees?

The European common toad has been seen sitting outside bee hives in early evening, waiting to catch the bees as they return. European common toads are quite stocky in appearance and the females can grow up to 7 inches/18 centimeters – the size of a man's hand. When mating, males hold onto the female's back to make sure they are in the right place when she lays her eggs, which are in the form of a long string.

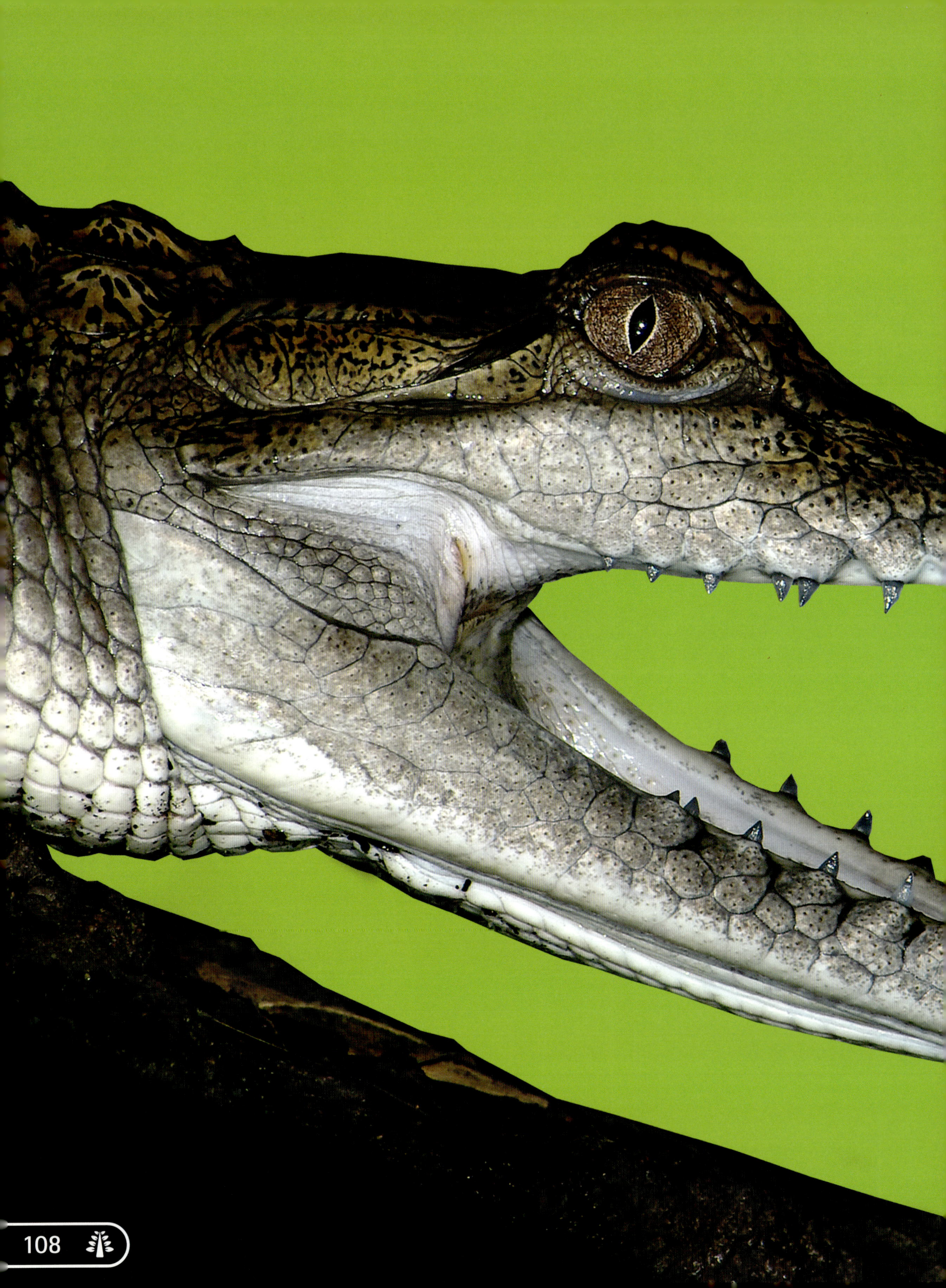

Reptiles

Reptiles are animals with tough, dry and scaly skin. They are cold-blooded, which means that it is difficult for them to control their own body temperature. They must rely on the temperature of their surroundings to warm up or cool down. For this reason, most reptiles live in warm climates, and spend much of their time basking in the sun.

All reptiles have backbones, including snakes and turtles. They breathe air so, even if they live in the sea, they have to come to the surface to breathe. There are about 6,000 different species of reptile, including crocodiles, alligators, lizards, chameleons, snakes, turtles and tortoises. Lizards are the largest group of reptiles with some 3,500 species. Most reptiles lay eggs with tough, rubbery shells, although a few species, including some snakes, give birth to live young.

Tortoises and turtles

Turtles and their close relations the tortoises and terrapins are some of the world's oldest reptiles. Giant turtles were swimming in the sea when dinosaurs were roaming on the land, over 65 million years ago. Today, there are about 240 different kinds of turtles, tortoises and terrapins. Tortoises live on dry land, terrapins swim in freshwater rivers and lakes, and turtles live in the oceans.

The biggest leatherback turtles can grow up to 10 feet/3 meters long, which is about the length of a small rowing boat. They can weigh up to 2,020lbs/916kg – about ten times more than an average man.

▼ How big are terrapins?

Terrapins are much smaller than turtles. The red-eared terrapin of North and South America grows to just 10 inches/25 centimeters long. It eats fish, insects and freshwater plants.

The red-eared terrapin is a sociable animal, living in large groups. It is active by day, and likes to spend time out of the water sunbathing on riverside roots or floating logs. Female terrapins lay clutches of up to 22 eggs, which hatch after about three months.

▲ Where do leatherback turtles live?

Leatherback turtles swim in warm seas around the world. Like all turtles, they spend their whole lives at sea. Female turtles come onto land when it is time to lay their eggs. Amazingly, they always come back to the beach where they hatched to do this.

When a female turtle has laid her eggs, she covers them with sand and returns to the ocean. Her parenting job is over. The sun warms the eggs until they hatch.

Do tortoises, turtles and terrapins have teeth? No. Instead they cut and tear their food with their sharp, beak-like jaws.

The shell of a tortoise, terrapin or turtle is made up of about 60 hard, bony plates, which cover the animal's back and underbelly. Only the head, tail and legs stick out from this protective armor.

A tortoise protects itself by drawing its head, legs and tail up inside its shell. It is very hard for a predator to beat this excellent defense tactic.

Where do Galapagos tortoises live?

Galapagos tortoises live on the Galapagos Islands, which are off the coast of Ecuador in the East Pacific Ocean. They grow up to 3 feet 6 inches/1.1 meters long, and males are usually bigger than females.

Large land tortoises such as the Galapagos tortoise grow very slowly. They can live for over 100 years, which is longer than most other kinds of animal.

▼ How do turtles breathe?

Turtles breathe air, just like land tortoises, but they can hold their breath underwater for up to two hours when they are resting. When sea turtles are active, they have to return to the surface to breathe every few minutes.

Hawksbill turtles swim in the Atlantic and Pacific Oceans. They stay fairly close to the shore, usually swimming in water no deeper than about 60 feet/18 meters. Hawksbills feed on sea grass and small marine animals.

Pythons and boas

All snakes are meat-eaters, but they kill their prey in a number of different ways. Constrictors do not use poison, but squeeze their prey to death. Boas and pythons are closely related to each other, and are both in the constrictor family of snakes. They coil themselves around their victims, squeezing more tightly each time the prey breathes out. Once the prey is dead, the snake swallows it whole.

Pythons open their jaws wide to eat their prey, usually swallowing it head-first. When a python swallows a very large animal, its ribs expand to fit the prey inside its body.

▲ Where do carpet pythons live?

Carpet pythons live in a variety of habitats in Australia. They are very adaptable, equally suited to life in the rainforest and in the desert. The carpet python preys on many different animals, including small marsupials, rodents and lizards.

Carpet pythons have an interesting pattern on their scaly skin, which looks like the design on an oriental carpet. This elaborate pattern provides good camouflage as the python lies in the shadows, waiting for its prey to pass by.

▼ Where do green tree pythons live?

Green tree pythons live in the rainforests of New Guinea. They look like the emerald tree boas of South America, and behave in the same way. Both types of snake sleep in trees during the day, and hunt for prey at night. Their green skin keeps them well hidden in their leafy habitat.

Adult green tree pythons are green but, when they first hatch out of their eggs, they are a bright yellow, and sometimes even red. After about a year they change color.

All snakes have long, scaly bodies, and slither about on their bellies as they have no legs. They are cold-blooded reptiles, which means they have to rely on the temperature of their surroundings to control their body heat.

Common boas grow to between 8 and 10 feet/2.4 and 3 meters long. Like all snakes, they never stop growing, and shed their skin regularly. The speed of growth slows down when they are adults.

How many species of snake are there?

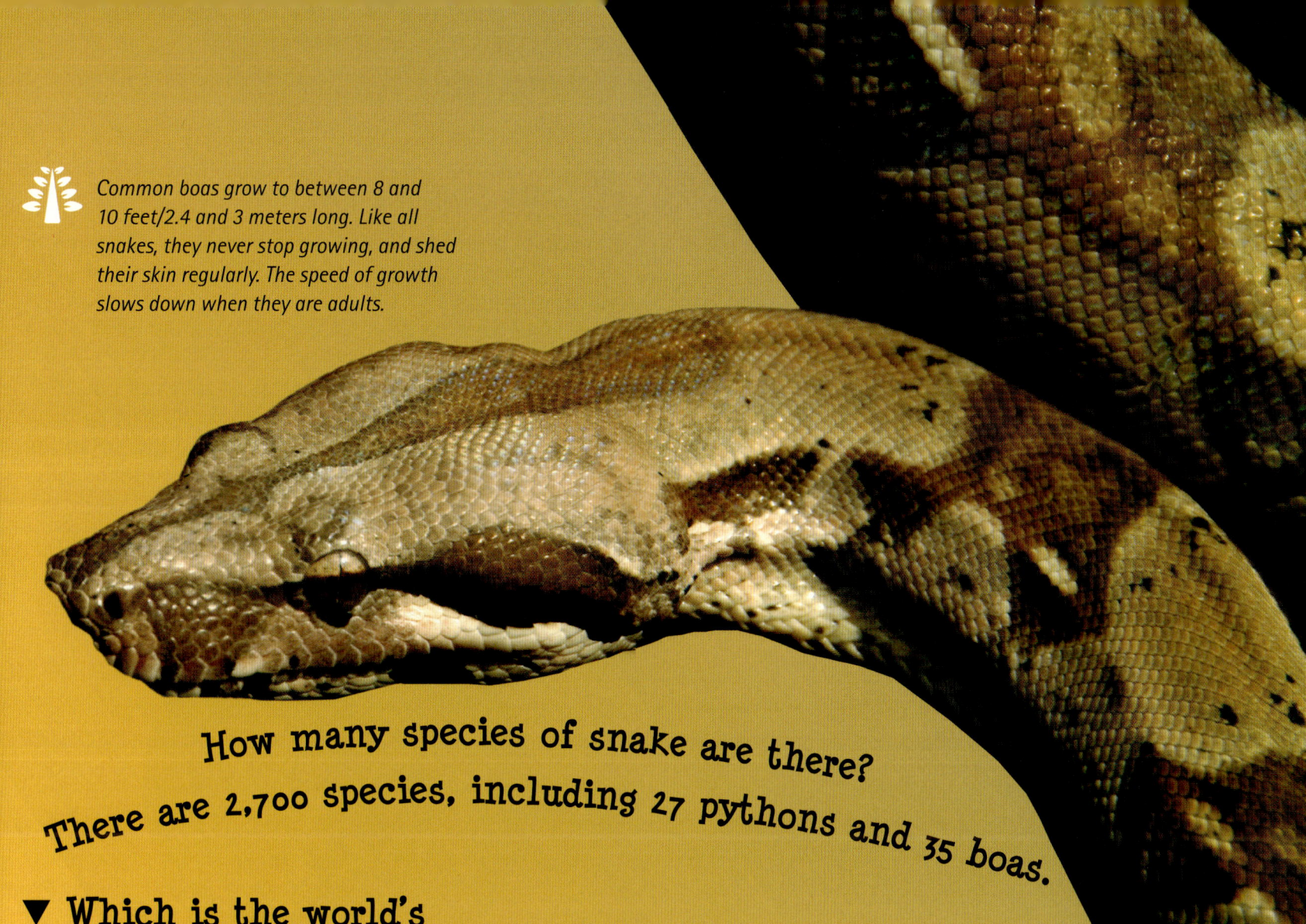

There are 2,700 species, including 27 pythons and 35 boas.

▼ Which is the world's heaviest snake?

The green anaconda of the South American rainforest is the heaviest snake in the world. This massive 29 feet 6 inches/9 meters long constrictor weighs about 500lbs/227kg – that's about 7 times heavier than an 11-year-old boy! The green anaconda can crush a caiman to death, then swallow it whole. It weighs more just after a meal like this.

Green anacondas are also known as 'water boas', as they spend much of their time near rivers. After a meal, an anaconda will bask in the sun while it digests its food.

Are common boas dangerous?

Common boas are also known as boa constrictors. They are not a danger to humans, as they would never be able to attack anything bigger than a bird or a bat.

Boa constrictors are found throughout South America, from Mexico to Argentina. They live in deserts, rainforests, grasslands and farmland.

Green anacondas can move faster in water than on land. They are good swimmers, spending a lot of time in the rivers of the South American rainforest.

Venomous snakes

About one-third of all species of snakes use poison to kill their prey. Many kinds of snake, including cobras and boomslangs, inject venom into their prey though sharp fangs. This venom is a neurotoxin which paralyzes the victim, so it can't fight or run away from the snake. Other snakes, including vipers, use a kind of poison that eats away at the flesh of its prey.

▼ Can snakes swim?

Many snakes are excellent swimmers, taking to the water to escape from predators or to cool off. Some species of snake actually live in the sea. There are over 50 species of sea snake, and some of them are extremely poisonous.

Sea snakes do not have gills like fish, so they can't breathe underwater. They can hold their breath for at least an hour at a time, but then they have to come up to the surface for some air. Sea snakes shed their skin more often than land snakes, about once every other week.

▼ Why do rattlesnakes rattle?

Rattlesnakes are named after the rattle on their tail, which they shake to warn off predators. A rattlesnake's poison is in its mouth, not in its tail. The most deadly rattlesnake in North America is the Mojave rattlesnake. One bite from this snake contains enough poison to kill 15,000 mice.

The eastern diamond-back rattlesnake is the biggest species of rattlesnake. At 8 feet 3 inches/2.5 meters long, it is about the length of a motorbike. When rattlesnakes shed their skin, they leave behind old scales on the tip of their tails. These dead scales rub together to make a rattling noise. The older a rattlesnake is, the louder its rattle.

Sea snakes swim in the warm waters of the south and western Pacific Ocean. Many have very strong venom in their hollow fangs, so they can overpower their prey before it swims away.

Rattlesnakes are vipers. All vipers have fangs at the front of their mouths, which inject poison into prey. The fangs fold back into its jaws, so the snake can shut its mouth.

Does a snake's poison kill everything? No, the poison usually works best on the animals it eats, while other animals may be immune.

114

When agitated, the Cape cobra rears up and flattens it neck so that its hood can be seen clearly. It hisses its warning, but this aggressive snake is quick to strike. Cape cobra venom causes respiratory failure in its prey.

Boomslangs can be dangerous, but they are only aggressive towards humans if they are frightened. A boomslang puffs up its throat as a warning if it is threatened.

▲ What are boomslangs?

Boomslangs belong to the colubrid snake family. All colubrids have teeth, but only a small number have rear fangs. Three-quarters of all snakes are colubrids, most of which are harmless, but boomslangs' venom is very toxic.

Like all snakes, boomslangs have very sharp senses, which help them to detect their prey. Boomslangs have large eyes, so they can see well in their African forest homes. They lunge at prey, such as birds, lizards and frogs, half swallowing it before delivering a deadly bite.

Why do cobras stand up?

Cobras are poisonous snakes that live in Asia and Africa. When they are threatened, they rise up from the ground and open out their hoods, to frighten predators away.

Some cobras, such as the Indian cobra, have hood markings that look like eyes. This confuses an attacker, giving the snake a chance to escape.

Devils, monsters and chameleons

Lizards are the biggest group of reptiles, with over 3,700 different species. They live in many kinds of habitat, in a range of climates. Most lizards love the warmth of tropical forests or dry deserts, but some more hardy species thrive in cooler mountain areas. Lizards vary in size, from the tiny 0.25 inch/16 millimeter geckos of the Dominican Republic in the Caribbean, to the giant 10 feet/ 3 meter Komodo dragons from Indonesia, in Southeast Asia.

▼ Why are thorny devils spiky?

The thorny devil lives in dry Australian bushland. This strange-looking lizard is covered in spines from nose to tail. The spines are only used in self-defense, and not to attack other animals. Predators are not keen on biting anything so sharp, and tend to leave the thorny devil alone.

Female thorny devils lay between 3 and 10 eggs in a nest, which take about four months to hatch. When the babies break their way out of the eggs, they look like miniature versions of their prickly parents.

For the first eight months of life, Komodo dragons live in forests, mainly to hide from predators and aggressive adults of their own species. Young Komodos soon grow too big to climb trees, and move into more open grassland.

The thorny devil eats ants, but only one at a time. It flicks out its tongue to lap up an ant, eating as many as 45 in a minute. Sometimes it will eat up to 1,500 ants at one meal.

Does the Komodo dragon hunt prey?

The Komodo dragon is a scavenger, often feasting on dead animals. However, this huge carnivore is also an active hunter. It uses its forked tongue to detect its prey, for example wild pigs or deer. Then it charges towards its victim, ripping it apart with its sharp teeth and strong jaws. Although the Komodo dragon is not venomous, its teeth contain such a toxic brew of bacteria on their surface that the prey quickly succumbs to infection and dies shortly after being bitten.

◀ Is the gila monster dangerous?

The gila monster is one of only two species of lizard with a poisonous bite. The other is the Mexican beaded lizard. Both these lizards live in the rocky desert of southern North America. The gila monster has bright red and black markings, to warn predators away. It will not attack humans, and only bites if threatened.

Like many desert animals, the gila monster is nocturnal, to keep out of the strong desert heat. It sleeps in a burrow or rocky crevice by day, emerging at night to hunt small rodents and to steal eggs from the nests of birds and reptiles.

A young gila monster can eat half its body weight in one meal. This ability to binge is important in a desert habitat, where food is hard to find.

Why do lizards bask in the sun? All lizards are cold-blooded and bask in the sun to control their body temperature.

▼ How do chameleons change color?

Chameleons change the color of their skin to blend in with their environment. This provides perfect camouflage from predators, such as boomslang snakes. Special cells in the chameleon's skin get bigger or smaller, which changes the reptile's color.

Most chameleons, for example the Jackson's chameleon, are between 6 and 14 inches/15 and 35 centimeters long. The smallest species, the pygmy chameleon, is just 1 inch/2.5 centimeters long – about as long as your thumb.

There are 100 species of chameleon, and most live in Madagascar, off the African coast. Chameleons' eyes are on cone-shaped turrets, which can move independently of each other.

Iguanas and geckos

Iguanas and geckos are two families of lizard that are found in warm climates around the world. They live in a variety of habitats – many iguana species live in tropical rainforests, but the unusual Galapagos marine iguana is well adapted to life by the sea, where it feeds on tiny marine algae. Some species of gecko, such as the leopard gecko, are found in dry, rocky deserts but, like iguanas, most geckos live in forests.

Flying geckos lay their eggs in trees. The eggs stick to the tree trunk with a natural glue.

▲ Can flying geckos really fly?

The flying gecko is a very unusual kind of lizard that lives in the rainforests of Southeast Asia. It has flaps of skin around its belly and in between its toes, which catch the air like a parachute as it glides between the branches of trees. The flying gecko can glide, but it can't actually fly like a bird. Flying geckos live for between three and eight years.

How well can geckos see? Geckos have excellent night vision, with big eyes that let in as much light as possible.

Green iguanas are excellent swimmers, and will drop into the water if threatened by a predator.

How big is the biggest iguana?

The green iguana is one of the biggest species of iguana. This common lizard grows over 6 feet 6 inches/2 meters in length, from head to tail. In the wild, the green iguana lives in the rainforests of Central and South America, but this species of lizard is sometimes kept as a pet. Think carefully before you buy one – they are hard to look after, and can live for up to 20 years.

▶ Where do geckos live?

Most lizards avoid people, but a few species of gecko are different, and are often found living in buildings. They eat insects, and are useful at getting rid of unwanted flies around the house. Their climbing skills mean they can walk upside down on ceilings!

There are about 850 species of gecko, and most of them are great climbers. Their feet have natural suction pads, which help them to grip onto flat surfaces as they climb, for example in between crevices on smooth rocks.

Most geckos are nocturnal but some, like the gold dust day gecko, are active during the day. These geckos eat insects and like to lick pollen, nectar and some soft fruits.

▼ What does the marine iguana look like?

Marine iguanas have flattened tails to help them steer in the water. Swishing their tails pushes them forwards as well as acting as a rudder.

Marine iguanas are dark gray or black in color, which helps them soak up as much of the sun's heat as possible after a cool swim. Marine iguanas dive to depths of up to 65 feet/ 20 meters and can stay underwater for up to 20 minutes. They survive the cold water by slowing down their heart rate, so they don't lose heat through the skin. After diving for food, marine iguanas bask in the sun to warm up again.

An adult marine iguana doesn't have many natural enemies in its remote habitat, on the volcanic Galapagos Islands, off the coast of Ecuador in South America. Hawks, owls and snakes are the main predators of young marine iguanas.

Slow worms, skinks and tuataras

Some families of lizard, for example the skink family, have a huge number of species. Other lizard families are much smaller, such as the anguid family, which only has about 100 species. Some lizards in the anguid family, the slow worms, look like snakes, but are actually a kind of lizard. There is one reptile, the tuatara, that looks like a lizard, but isn't one at all. The tuatara is an ancient species that belongs to a reptile group all of its own.

▼ Where do five-lined skinks live?

Five-lined skinks, named after the five stripes down their bodies, are found in the USA, preferring to live in a moist, woody habitat. During cold winter months, they hibernate in woodpiles and rock crevices to conserve their energy.

Compared to many lizards, five-lined skinks are excellent parents. A female five-lined skink lays up to 18 marble-sized eggs in a warm, damp nest, often in a rotting woodpile. She defends her eggs from predators, but abandons her babies a day or so after they hatch.

Tuataras develop slowly and may take as long as 20 years to reach adulthood. It is believed they may live as long as 100 years.

▲ How old are tuataras?

The tuatara is the last remaining member of an extinct family of reptiles that walked the Earth at the same time as dinosaurs. Today, tuataras are only found on a few small islands off the coast of New Zealand. They are one of the most endangered animals in the world.

Tuataras are cold-blooded creatures, like all other reptiles, and have a very low body temperature. This makes them do things very slowly, for example chew their food. A tuatara may fall asleep in the middle of a meal! This slow-moving reptile eats insects, small lizards, eggs and chicks.

Young five-lined skinks have brightly colored tails, which break off if they are grabbed, allowing the skink to escape.

The broad-headed skink takes its name from its triangular-shaped head. It lives in the humid forests in North America.

What is a skink?

The skink family is the largest group of lizard, with over 1,300 different species. Most skinks have small, shiny scales, with long, tube-shaped bodies and short legs. They are active by day, foraging for insects and plants.

True to its name, the blue-tongued skink has a vivid blue tongue, which it sticks out at predators to frighten them away. In self-defense, this skink puffs up its body to appear bigger and scarier, and will hiss very loudly.

Where do skinks live? Skinks live on every continent of the world, except Antarctica. They are most common in the deserts of Australia.

One way to tell a slow worm from a snake is to look at its eyes. Slow worms have eyelids, but snakes don't.

▶ How does the slow worm move?

A slow worm is a kind of legless lizard, which moves by wriggling along the ground. Slow worms grow up to 2 feet/60 centimeters long, and live in fields and scrubland in Europe, North Africa and Southeast Asia. They hibernate during the winter.

Like many species of lizard, slow worms feed on insects, spiders, and other small invertebrates. They have excellent senses of hearing and smell, which help them locate their prey.

Crocodiles and alligators

Crocodiles and alligators belong to a group of reptiles called the crocodilians. These fierce carnivores have not changed much for millions of years, since they hunted in prehistoric swamps while the dinosaurs walked the Earth. Today, there are 14 species of crocodile, two species of alligator and six species of caiman. There is just one more species, the Indian gharial, which looks different from the others, with a long, slender snout.

The eyes and nostrils of all crocodilians are high on their heads, so they can see and breathe while most of their bodies are underwater.

When baby crocodiles hatch out of their eggs, they call out for their mother. Just like a newborn human baby, a baby crocodile needs to make a noise to get attention.

▶ How do crocodiles care for their young?

Crocodiles make much better parents than many other reptiles. A female Nile crocodile lays up to 75 eggs, burying them under sand in the riverbank. She guards them for about 3 months until they hatch, then carries them gently in her big mouth down to the water. She goes on protecting them from predators for another few weeks, before leaving them to fight their own battles.

Crocodiles devour small prey whole, but they rip up the flesh of larger prey, such as deer, before they eat it. They can't chew their food, so they swallow stones, which grind their food inside their bellies, mashing it into a pulp. They do not need to eat often, only having a big meal about once a week.

▲ What do caimans eat?

Caimans look like alligators, but they are smaller, with shorter snouts. However, their jaws are still wide enough to be able to hunt a variety of prey, such as fish, birds, lizards and small mammals. They usually hunt at night, swallowing their prey whole in the dark.

Many caimans live in the warm, tropical rivers of Central and South America. Some are found on islands in the Caribbean. Caribbean caimans' ancestors probably swam there, or drifted on ocean currents, from the South American mainland.

Where does the gharial like to hunt?

The gharial hunts in fast-flowing rivers, where there are plenty of fish to catch in its long, thin jaws. This specialized fish hunter is found in India and Pakistan, swimming in large rivers, such as the Ganges and the Indus.

Unlike its bulkier crocodilian relatives, the gharial has weak legs and can't walk well or easily on land. It spends nearly all its life in the water, but will haul itself onto the riverbank to rest and bask in the sun.

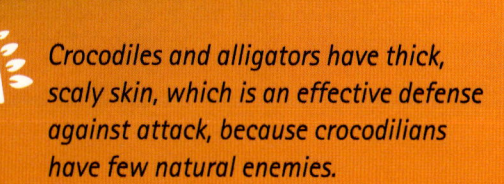

Crocodiles and alligators have thick, scaly skin, which is an effective defense against attack, because crocodilians have few natural enemies.

Which crocodile is the biggest? The saltwater crocodile is. It grows up to 20 feet/6 meters long. That's about twice as long as a speedboat!

▼ How fast are alligators?

Alligators, such as the American alligator, can run fast on land, but they are even quicker in the water. To swim, they tuck their legs under their bodies and swish their strong tails from side to side, powering themselves through the water.

The American alligator lives in southeastern USA, in warm rivers and swamps. It will eat almost anything it can catch, including water birds, fish and turtles. In populated areas, the American alligator will sometimes ambush farm animals that have strayed too close to the water.

You can tell alligators and crocodiles apart by their teeth. When an alligator shuts its mouth, you can't see any teeth in its bottom jaw. When a crocodile has its mouth closed, you can see the fourth tooth on each side of its bottom jaw.

Birds

Birds are animals with feathers, claws, bills and beaks, and most are capable of flight. They have developed several features that enable them to fly, including light, strong and flexible wings, hollow bones, slim legs and beaks instead of jaws and teeth. Birds lay eggs with hard shells to protect the developing young. Most birds look after their young, bringing them food and caring for them in a cosy nest.

A bird's feathers help it to keep warm, as well as to fly. The wings curve in an airfoil shape from the front to the back, generating lift when flapped, pulling the animal up into the air and keeping it moving forwards. Tails can be used for a variety of steering and braking manoeuvres in the air.

As flight requires a lot of energy, birds have very high metabolic rates – which means their bodies can convert food into energy very quickly. As a result, their average body temperature is up to 5 degrees higher than other warm-blooded animals. Birds' hearts also beat very quickly: a robin's heart, for example, beats at 600 times a minute, compared to a human heartbeat of 60 beats a minute. This is to get oxygen and energy around the body as quickly as possible.

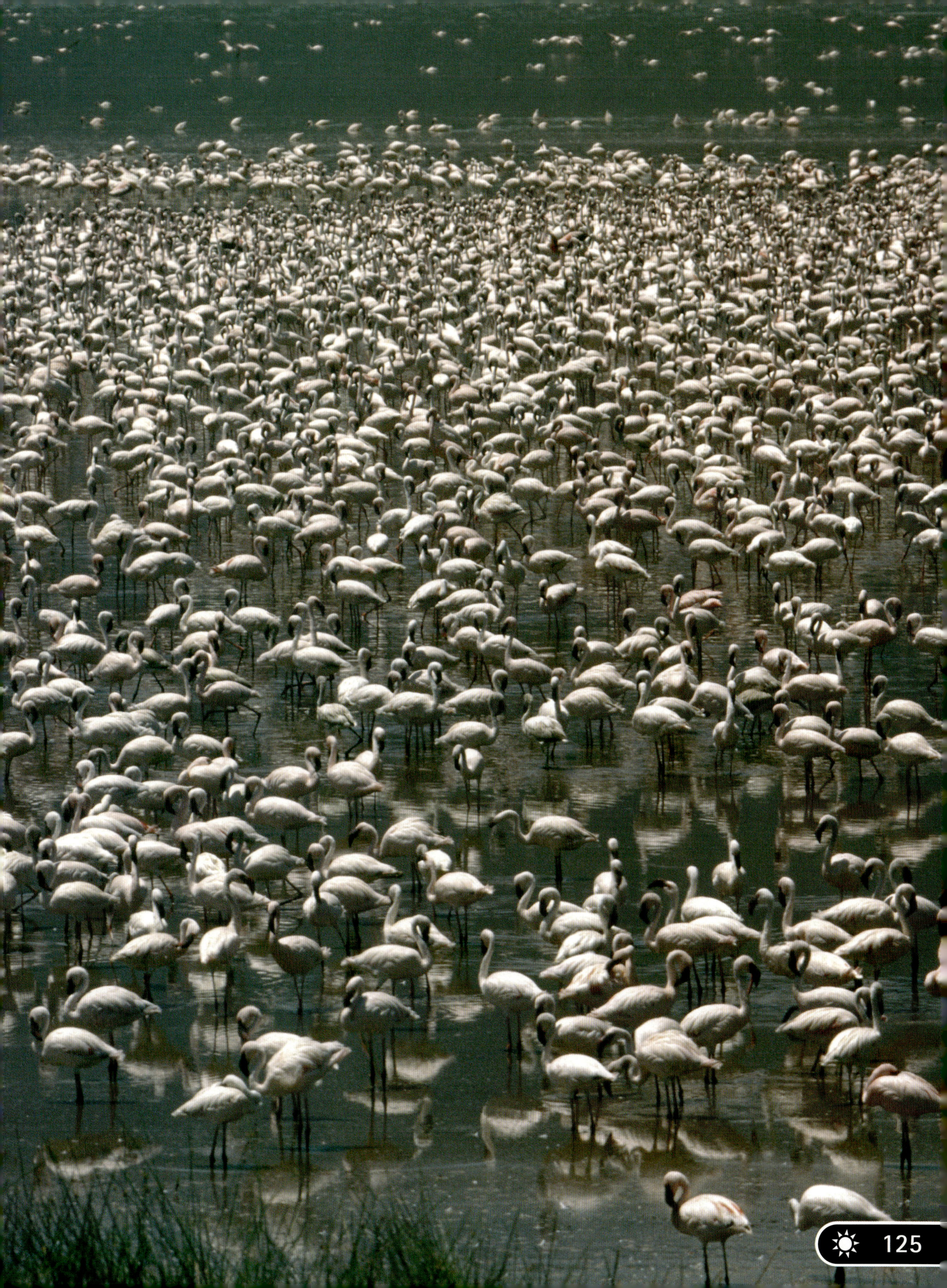

Flightless birds

Of the roughly 9,000 species of bird, around 40 are flightless. It is thought that flightless birds are all descended from birds that could fly at one time or another, and that they have lost the ability over time. This could be due to changes in habitat, lack of natural predators, or a specialization in other forms of travel, such as fast running or skilful swimming.

▼ Why can't an ostrich fly?

In short, because it is too big! The ostrich is the biggest bird on the planet. It reaches 9 feet/2.75 meters in height and weighs about 260lbs/120kg. Scientists have calculated that no bird over about 40lbs/18kg would be able to fly, because their muscle power could never be enough to get them airborne. Ostriches are fast runners, reaching speeds of up to 45 miles/70 kilometers an hour.

▼ How does a little spotted kiwi find food?

Like other kiwis, the little spotted kiwi of New Zealand finds its prey by smell, using nostrils on the end of its beak. Its food includes small insects and worms. Like many other flightless birds, the kiwi is threatened with extinction because of the introduction of predators such as domestic cats and pigs. In New Zealand, they have vanished from the main island and are clinging on in more sheltered island habitats in the seas around the area.

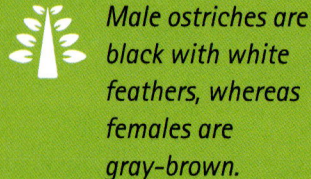

Male ostriches are black with white feathers, whereas females are gray-brown.

Although small, the little spotted kiwi lays the largest egg for its body size – it is a quarter of an adult's weight.

◀ How deep can an emperor penguin dive?

Although they are a little unsteady on land, emperor penguins are expert swimmers and can dive to depths of up to 820 feet/250 meters searching for fish. They are also capable of huge feats of endurance. Over three winter months in the Antarctic, one of the coldest places on earth, the male emperor penguin shelters his egg on his feet, protecting it from the ice.

The emperor is the world's largest penguin and stands at up to 4 feet/1.2 meters high – about the height of a six-year-old child.

Where does the emu live?

The emu lives in Australia and is the second largest bird in the world. Emu eggs are a dark green color when they are first laid, but darken to a glossy black within a few days. A female can lay up to 10 eggs, each one weighing about 1lbs 8oz/700g – that's heavier than a grapefruit. The male incubates the eggs for about eight weeks, until the young chicks hatch. Their brown and white striped coloring provides camouflage.

How fast can an emu run? It can reach speeds of 30 miles/50 kilometers an hour.

An emu's booming call can be heard over 1 mile/1.6 kilometers away.

Game birds

Game birds are adapted to living on the ground. They all have shorter legs, shorter bills and generally feed on plants, seeds and other vegetable matter. The young of many species, however, tend to eat only insects. In general, males perform displays to attract females, but play no part in rearing their young, although there are exceptions. Many species are timid and are colored in camouflaging tones. A number are popular quarry for hunters.

▼ When do willow grouse change color?

Willow grouse change color for the winter and summer. They are red-brown in summer, with a red patch over the eye for males and a white belly. With the onset of winter, they molt their brown coat in favor of an all-white camouflage. One part that doesn't change, however, is their black tails. They are a thick-set, round-bodied, chicken-shaped bird that eats by plucking shoots and leaves from the ground on European moors and heaths.

What do gray partridges eat?

Adult partridges eat seeds, leaves, grass and plant shoots but, during their first weeks of life, the young feed on insects. The additional protein that the insects provide is important for the early stages of their growth.

Gray partridges usually nest on the ground under the cover of a hedge or other tall plants.

☀ *Willow grouse is regularly shot for sport but is not as extensively farmed and released as pheasant.*

☀ *The gray partridge has the largest average clutch size of any bird at 15-19 eggs.*

◀ When do quails fly?

Not very often – they don't seem to like it, preferring to run from danger instead. When startled, they will fly in a short burst, making a low arc before dropping back to the ground. However, quail breed in southern Europe and spend the winter in Africa, so are quite capable of long flights.

The shy quails are most often spotted when migrating, when they take rests in open fields.

How many feathers are there in a peacock's tail? Up to 150.

▶ Where do peacocks live in the wild?

The peacock's natural habitat is in India, where it is an open forest bird that feeds on plants, insects, spiders, lizards and sometimes frogs. It nests on the ground or roosts in trees. Males have huge, spectacularly colored tail feathers which they fan out and shake to impress females. Females have more muted coloring, of brown and white feathers, adding to their camouflage when they nest on the ground. Peafowl are a relative of the pheasant, which also have long tails.

The male peafowl has a loud and piercing call and is sometimes used as a 'guard dog' to warn off strangers.

129

Waterfowl

Waterfowl are birds that spend a large portion of their lives over, in, or using the water, either swimming or hunting. They have webbed feet to help them swim. They may also often have extra-waterproof feathers and, in many cases, specially adapted bills rather than beaks. They use a number of hunting techniques – diving, bobbing or herding – to catch the fish that they eat.

▼ What are the most common water birds?

Ducks and geese are perhaps the most familiar water birds. The mallard is the most widespread. In the winter, the male has his famous metallic green head, but in summer this turns brown, known as 'eclipse' plumage. The females are brown and build down-lined nests on the ground or on slightly raised sites in which to lay their eggs. Their brown coloring provides camouflage for the female.

Mallards are found throughout the northern hemisphere and have been introduced to Australia and New Zealand.

▼ How deep can a white-breasted cormorant dive?

White-breasted cormorants dive from the surface with a slight jump, and can go as deep as 33 feet/10 meters for up to 30-40 seconds. A cormorant's feathers do not trap air in the same way that those of other birds do, and this allows them to dive more quickly and chase their prey underwater. They also have a hooked beak, well adapted for grasping and digging into fish. Underwater, they can propel themselves with their large webbed feet.

The white-breasted cormorant lives around the coast of Africa where it dives for fish, eels and crustaceans.

☀ The albatross lays the heaviest egg of any seabird. It can weigh over 1lbs 1oz/500g.

◄ Where do albatrosses nest?

Wandering albatrosses nest on small remote islands far out in the Southern Ocean. They prefer windswept areas, where the currents help them launch themselves into the air. Albatrosses use their huge wings to glide long distances on strong air currents, hardly beating their wings at all. In fact, they use far more energy in take off and landing. They feed mainly on squid and cuttlefish, sometimes diving under the water to catch their food.

How large is an Australian pelican's beak?

The Australian pelican's bill is the largest in the world and can reach up to a whopping 18 inches/47 centimeters. What's most distinctive about the pelican bill, apart from its size, is the large pouch beneath it. Pelicans hunt in a group, herding fish into shallow water to be scooped into their bills. Pelicans are graceful flyers too, often holding tight V formations or swirling around in packs.

How much water can a pelican's bill hold? 32 pints/15 liters – more than his belly can!

☀ Male and female pelicans co-operate in building their nests. The male brings the material and the female heaps it up to form a simple structure.

Shore birds

Most shore birds have elongated toes to stop them sinking into the mud. They are usually long-legged and long-billed. Some beaks are straight, others are curved. Those that are curved are normally curved downwards. They all tend to feed around water – some preferring rocky shores, some preferring sandy beaches, and others choosing muddy shallows or boggy marshes. Large groups of waders gather at high tides to feed at the water's edge.

Why do herons change color?

In the spring, many herons develop bright patterns on their legs and bills. Their facial skin may even 'blush' slightly during courtship. These changes indicate that they are ready to breed. Like all herons, gray herons are primarily fish-eaters, but they will eat almost anything they can catch, including rats and frogs. They patiently watch their prey, attacking with a precise stab.

▶ Where do you find flamingos?

Flamingos are scattered all over the world, from southeastern Europe to Southeast Asia, Africa and Central America. Like most flamingos, the greater flamingo nests in large colonies. They build up their nests from the mud on low-lying islands. These nests are vulnerable to flooding or, sometimes, to a drop in the water levels that allows predators to get closer over dry land. Some years they raise very few young, while other years there are 'baby booms' that maintain their population.

▼ Why do curlews have long bills?

The curlew's long, down-curved bill is specially adapted to probe into wet mud for worms, insects, crabs and mollusks that may live there. Curlews prefer shorelines and inland waters such as marshes and heath bogs, and can also be seen poking about in rock pools. They form flocks in the winter months and, in Europe in the spring, their song is one of the most attractive – accelerating into a bubbling trill after a 'cur-lew' sound after which they are named.

Curlews nest in shallow hollows that they line with grass and lay dark, speckled eggs that are camouflaged to look like a stone.

Flamingos are the only 'filter-feeding' birds, which means they filter the water for food.

The gray heron is Europe's largest heron, with a wingspan of up to 5 feet 7 inches/1.7 meters.

How many avocets do you get in a flock?
They can be tens of thousands strong – the population of a whole town.

Male avocets have a larger, squared black wing tip than the females.

▶ **What's special about an avocet's bill?**

Avocets' bills turn upwards towards the end. If they find the right conditions, such as shallow salt water and oozing mud with drier islands scattered about, they will form larger, sprawling colonies, rather than packing tightly together like some other birds. But avocets are sociable and don't mind each other's company. They even jostle each other when feeding without too much irritation. When it feeds, the avocet leans forward on its long, blue-gray legs and sweeps its bill sideways through the water in order to find and catch small shrimp and marine worms.

Birds of prey

Many birds of prey, such as eagles and hawks, are strong hunters with large forward-facing eyes that can sometimes see animals such as rabbits from as far away as 2 miles/3.2 kilometers and are good at judging distances. They have hooked, powerful bills to tear open flesh and strong feet with sharp talons to catch prey. They are also often fast and skilful fliers and spend a lot of their time in the air.

▼ How do red kites fly?

Red kites are very light, agile fliers with a large, typically forked tail for manoeuvrability. In flight, the red kite flexes its wings and twists its long tail from side to side to use air currents to their fullest, although it doesn't usually go too high. It is also capable of fast stoops and twisting dives. Like the golden eagle, it also scavenges dead meat from sheep or rabbits, and will eat earthworms or insects.

Peregrines nest on broad ledges or scrapes on cliffs or quarries, but some people have found them – very rarely – on window ledges.

Red kites take their name from the red-rust coloring on their forked tails and forewings.

◄ How does a peregrine falcon hunt?

Peregrines mainly hunt other birds ranging in sizes from a starling or pigeon to a grouse. They are extremely fast and probably reach speeds higher than any other bird when dive-bombing their prey from above. As they dive, they fold in their wings and then reach out their claws on impact, sometimes catching them in mid-flight, other times striking them to the ground. They also approach birds from below or chase them in a level flight with acrobatic mid-air displays.

▶ How big is a golden eagle?

Golden eagles are powerful birds of prey that have large wingspans of over 7 feet 3 inches/2.2 meters and can weigh as much as 15lbs/6.7kg when adult. Despite their size they can soar with great grace. Golden eagles use their powerful vision to scan the sky for birds, and the ground below for rabbits, dead sheep, grouse and hares. Immature golden eagles can be identified by their black, slightly scruffy-looking feathers. Adults have a paler, tawny head and dark brown plumage.

Golden eagles can live for 25 years. The female lays between one and three eggs in February to June.

How fast is a peregrine falcon? Diving, it can reach 117 miles/188 kilometers an hour!

The kestrel can be found almost everywhere across the whole of Europe.

Which bird of prey is most common in towns?

Kestrels are one of the most commonly seen birds of prey in Europe and they are often spotted on telegraph poles or wire. Kestrels hover in mid-air, as they scan the ground for the voles, beetles, earthworms and small birds that make up their diet. They fan their tails and beat their wings rapidly to keep in one spot. They also use their tails as a wind-break when they land.

Parrots

Most parrots have large heads, short necks and short legs and many have brightly colored feathers. Their most identifiable feature is their bill, which has a broad base and a chisel-shaped cutting edge for cracking open seeds. Parrots also use their feet to hold and manipulate their food while eating.

▼ Which cockatoo gathers in huge flocks?

In Australia, large flocks of up to 2,000 sulphur-crested cockatoos can gather to forage on grass, seeds, sprouting wheat, maize and other grain. These flocks use a 'sentinel' warning system, which means that, as the flock feeds, several individuals act as lookouts and raise the alarm if danger approaches by making loud screeches and raising the yellow crests on their heads. These cockatoos can damage crops and are considered pests by farmers. They also feed on nuts, berries, blossoms and insect larvae, holding food with the foot and attacking or opening it with the powerful bill.

Cockatoos form mating pairs and share the incubation of eggs in their tree hollow for 30 days.

▼ What is a parakeet?

Parakeets are small or medium-sized parrots. The ring-necked parakeet, like many, is very adaptable. It lives in tropical Africa and Asia, where it can be found in a variety of woodland types, mangroves, open farmland, savannah grassland and sometimes even parks and gardens. Like most parrots, parakeets often gather together in large groups and can cause damage to crops. Males have a blue, gray and black coloring on their necks and cheeks, plus the rose-pink collar from which they take their name.

Ring-necked parakeets can be very noisy and annoying to those that live nearby.

▶ Where do budgerigars live in the wild?

In the wild, budgerigars live in semi-arid areas of Australia. They have a nomadic lifestyle, which means they move from place to place throughout the year and follow a general seasonal pattern of moving north in winter and south in summer. They breed at any time of the year, usually when there is a good supply of food. The birds nest in small hollows in tree trunks and sometimes share these with other couples.

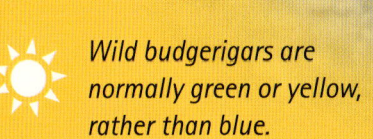

Wild budgerigars are normally green or yellow, rather than blue.

Fossils of parrot-like birds date back to 40 million years ago. How old are parrots?

Macaws are the largest parrots and the scarlet macaw is the most numerous, but is under threat.

Why do parrots eat soil and clay?

Scarlet macaws, like many types of parrot, gather near riverbanks in Central and South America to eat clay. It is thought that the birds gain vital minerals from the clay or it may neutralize the toxic affects of poisons from plants they have eaten, or both. Some Australian parrots have even been found with charcoal in their stomachs.

Nocturnal birds

There are many types of nocturnal birds including owls, nightjars and frogmouths. All these birds hunt at night, and have very soft wing feathers which allow them to fly silently. Owls have a rounded facial disk, made of short, stiff feathers, and big eyes on the front of their heads. This gives them excellent vision and depth perception. Nightjars' and frogmouths' eyes are on each side of their heads.

▼ Do owls only come out at night?

Owls usually hunt at night, but may change their behavior under certain pressures. Barn owls can sometimes be seen during the day in winter, and often hunt before dark in summer, especially if they have young to feed. Barn owls nest in holes in trees or in buildings and lay four to seven eggs between May and June. They are found throughout Europe, although they are not common, and eat voles, mice, rats and occasionally small birds.

Like the barn owl, the tawny owl lives with its mate.

Which is the owl which hoots after dark?

The tawny owl makes the familiar hooting sound, but it can also make other, yapping sounds and these are more often heard through the year. Tawny owls live in woods and nest in a hole in a tree or in buildings, but may take an old stick nest left by a crow or magpie. They carry their food in their beaks, unlike other birds of prey, which carry it in their talons.

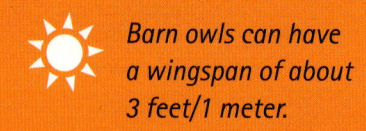

Barn owls can have a wingspan of about 3 feet/1 meter.

▶ Where do nightjars make their nest?

Nightjars nest on the ground, where they scrape a clear patch in which to sit. They hunt insects and catch them in mid-flight using a broad, wide-open gaping beak. Nightjars hunt at dusk or dawn, when their distinctive, long 'churr' call can be heard. They have camouflaged coloring similar to dead leaves or bark, which can make them very difficult to spot.

How long do tawny owls live? Up to ten years.

☀ The nightjar is a solitary bird and does not gather in flocks.

☀ Tawny frogmouths mate for life and usually use the same nest each year, making repairs when needed.

◀ What is a frogmouth?

Frogmouths, like the tawny frogmouth, are related to nightjars. They live in forests or open woodlands and spend their days resting in a tree trunk, where they are well camouflaged. At night, frogmouths ambush any prey that comes close to them from perches close to or even on the ground. They eat mainly insects, but sometimes catch lizards, frogs and mice.

Swifts and hummingbirds

Swifts and their relatives, hummingbirds, are extremely agile flyers. Swifts spend years on the wing, eating, drinking and even sleeping without the need to land. Their narrow bodies and long, stiff wings are aerodynamically ideal for prolonged flights. Hummingbirds have perfected the art of hovering in front of flowers to sip the nectar. Swifts and hummingbirds can migrate long distances, in some cases up to thousands of miles.

▼ How do hummingbirds hover?

Like all hummingbirds, the horned sun gem can twist its wings in a figure of eight. As well as hovering, this allows them to fly both forwards and backwards. They can also fly up, down, sideways and, incredibly, even upside down for short distances. The horned sun gem lives in forests and woodlands in Bolivia and central and eastern Brazil. It feeds on the nectar of flowering bushes and trees as well as small insects.

Hummingbirds have the fastest wingbeat of all birds. They fly at 90 wingbeats a second – that's over 5,000 a minute!

What is the smallest bird in the world?

Hummingbirds are the smallest birds in the world and, of these, the bee humming bird is the smallest. It is found in coastal forests and forest edges in Cuba, as well as in mountain valleys, swamps and gardens. Like all hummingbirds, it feeds mainly on the nectar of flowers and very small insects. It was once common throughout Cuba, but now, as with so many other species, it is rare and localized as a result of habitat destruction and change.

How do white-throated needle-tail swifts mate?

Little is known about the breeding behavior of the white-throated needle-tails, but it is thought that mating takes place during flight, and courtship displays consist of a series of vertical flights. Needle-tails lay their eggs on a platform of sticks placed in a hollow or similar crevice high in a tall conifer.

Which bird is almost the size of a nut?

It is the bee hummingbird, which is only 2.3 inches/6 centimeters long!

▼ Where do swifts nest?

Swifts used to nest mainly on cliffs and in trees, but many have now become reliant on buildings as good nesting locations. They arrive in Europe late in spring and leave for Africa in early autumn. Flocks may fly very high or at rooftop level. They build feather-lined nests in deep holes, often in roof spaces, out of feathers snatched in flight which they mix with saliva. They lay up to three eggs between May and June.

When they leave their nest, young swifts spend up to four years in constant flight before breeding themselves.

Toucans and hornbills

There are over 50 species of hornbill. They take their name from their large, curved beak, which is often topped by a hard, smooth shield. Hornbills are found in Africa, across India and Asia to Papua New Guinea. In the Amercias, toucans occupy a similar niche. There are about 40 species. They also have large beaks, but theirs are brightly colored, and do not have a shield or 'casque'.

▼ How do toucans fly?

Toucans, like the emerald toucanet, seem to have a haphazard way of flying, with short bursts of flapping, followed by a rest. This gives them an up-and-down flight path. They do not fly long distances, preferring to hop between tree branches. The emerald toucanet lives in mountainous forests and open woodlands of South America.

Rainbow-billed toucans live in the rainforests of South America, from Mexico to Venezuela and Columbia.

Like all toucans, emerald toucanets live in pairs or small groups.

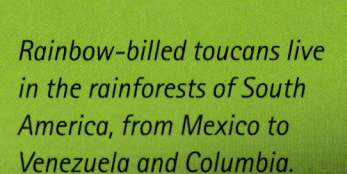

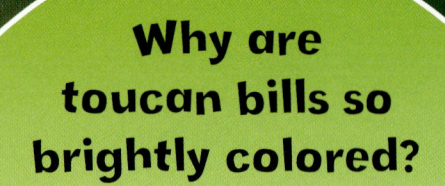

Why are toucan bills so brightly colored?

No one really knows! It may help species recognize each other, as they all have their own distinctive patterns. The rainbow-billed toucan's is one of the most brightly colored bills of all, with brown, green, blue, orange and yellow markings. Toucans' bills are made of keratin – the same material as fingernails and hair – and are strong but light in weight.

Can the helmeted hornbill laugh?

It certainly sounds like it – their calls are like hoots of hysterical laughter. Helmeted hornbills live in the Malay peninsular, Borneo and Sumatra. They use their bills to dislodge rotten bark from tree trunks to get at insects and other small animals, but they mainly eat figs and other fruit. Male helmeted hornbills may fight over territory, flying directly at their opponents and ramming them with their bills.

For how long do greater Indian hornbills live?

Hornbills are fairly long-lived birds, with some living for 30-40 years.

The helmeted hornbill lives on the Malay peninsula, Borneo and Sumatra.

▶ How do greater Indian hornbills nest?

Like many birds, the greater Indian hornbill nests in a hollow in a tree to raise its young, safe from predators. Once a female is in the nest, the male hornbill seals the entrance up with mud. Safe inside, the female incubates the eggs, while her partner feeds her through a small hole. After about three months, when the eggs have hatched and the young hornbills are ready to leave the nest, the female breaks out of her muddy home.

The greater Indian hornbills mate for life and raise one or two young at a time.

143

Perching birds

Perching birds form a large order of birds known as 'passeriforms' which contains more than half of all known bird species. Most of these birds have slim, long toes that can grip well and lock together for security when perching on branches high up in trees. Most of these birds invest time and energy in raising their young, which are often blind and helpless when they hatch.

▼ What is a martin?

Martins spend much of their time flying through the air catching flying insects. Their feet are very small but are still strong enough to perch with, unlike swallows. House martins are most famous for building nests of saliva and mud in people's roof spaces. In some parts of Europe, they still nest in more remote places such as high mountain ledges. European birds often spend the winter in Africa.

A house martin's small, open nest is usually home to four or five chicks at a time.

What kind of bird is a robin?

European robins are part of a group of perching birds called thrushes. They are generally quite stout, solid-built birds with large heads, big eyes and short, strong bills. Robins live mainly in forests and woodland areas all over Europe and they have become highly adapted to follow larger animals as they rummage around the forest floor, churning up the mud. Robins then pick out the worms and insects which have been exposed.

Robins build domed nests of grasses and leaves, often in hedges, bushes or thick ivy. They line them with moss and animal hair.

▶ What is an oven bird?

Oven birds are a type of bird found in Central America, so named because of the way they build their nests. They collect mud, straw or dung, which they mix with saliva to make a nest in trees or on man-made objects such as posts or telegraph poles. These nests look like a type of oven found in South America. The nests are impressive buildings with two chambers – one enclosed for containing and protecting the chicks, with a spiralling passageway that leads outside to an entrance that usually faces away from the wind.

The oven bird is the national bird of Argentina.

How many ticks does an oxpecker eat in one day? Oxpeckers can pick off around 100 ticks each day.

▶ Why do oxpeckers peck at oxen?

Oxpeckers are useful birds for larger mammals as they pick lice and other parasites out of their fur or skin. They also remove skin and body fluids – sometimes even earwax or snot – as well as cleaning around the edges of wounds. Oxpeckers have short legs and sharp claws which enable them to cling onto the fur or hide of the mammal, even if it is moving about. Oxpeckers are sociable birds that feed in flocks and return to communal roosts at night.

Oxpeckers build nests lined with animal hair in holes in trees, and lay two to three eggs.

145

Song birds

To some extent, all birds are song birds. All birds make some form of noise or sound for a variety of reasons. These can range from more simple 'calls' like that of the cuckoo or pigeon, which are closely related to perching birds, to the more complex 'songs' of warblers. Their songs, like all birdsong, are created using a 'syrinx', which is a sound box located in their necks, a little bit like our voicebox. However, it can pass air through two separate channels at once, producing different noises simultaneously. Birds change the pitch and volume by tightening and relaxing muscles in their necks.

Nightingales are commonly believed to have one of the finest singing voices and their song has inspired poets.

▼ Where do canaries live?

Canaries are a type of finch famous for their singing voices. Originally from the Azores, Madeira and the Canary Islands, canaries are now popular pets all over the world. In the wild, canaries nest in orchards, or in trees and bushes. They have brown and grey streaks to their coloring, rather than the all-yellow of their captive cousins. They were first bred as pets by monks in the 1600s. Originally only males were sold, as they were more in demand for their singing voices.

The canary can take 30 mini-breaths a second to replenish its air supply when singing.

◄ Do nightingales sing at night?

Nightingales are usually heard at dawn or dusk between the months of April and August, occasionally breaking into bursts of song during the day. They don't really sing during the night, but they can sometimes be heard just before night falls. Nightingales usually hide in thick undergrowth and vegetation close to the ground, where they search for worms, insect larvae, beetles and berries.

▶ How many species of warbler are there?

There are around 400 species of warbler and most tend to migrate to breed. Their arrival in Europe coincides with the annual insect population increase in early summer, so there is plenty of food with which to feed their young. Warblers have probing beaks for picking caterpillars and aphids from bark and leaves, and for foraging for berries, spiders and insects. Female marsh warblers lay six small, slightly camouflaged eggs in nests that hang from tall stems in dense vegetation.

The marsh warbler is the bird with the most songs, with 84 different variations or mimicked sounds.

When do most birds sing?
At dawn – although exactly why is not fully understood.

What does the red-eyed vireo's song sound like?

The red-eyed vireo can sometimes sound like it is endlessly repeating the same question and answer over and over again. Vireos are similar to warblers but with heavier bills. They breed mainly in North America, where they sometimes fall victim to a bullying bird called the brown-headed cowbird. This is a nest parasite that lays its eggs in other birds' nests so the victims raise the chick as their own.

The red-eyed vireo can sing its song thousands of times over the course of a day.

Weavers and creepers

Weaver birds are renowned for building elaborate nests. They have rounded, conical bills and eat mainly seeds. Most breed in Africa, although there are also species in tropical Asia and in Australia. Creepers are small woodland or mountain birds with thin, pointed, down-curved bills. They nest in small, makeshift holes near to where they feed. All find their food by creeping or climbing on rocks or trees.

Wall creepers build quite untidy nests, mostly deep in gaps between rubble and rocks.

▲ Why do wall creepers creep on walls?

The natural habitat of the wall creeper is mountains and gorges, to which they are extremely well adapted. They sometimes descend from their mountain homes in winter and may be seen clambering on the walls of buildings. Wall creepers have long claws for grabbing onto hard rock and a long, slim, slightly down-curved bill for probing around damp rocky crevices for spiders and insects.

How many wild red-billed queleas are there? Estimates put their population at more than 1.5 billion.

How many red-billed queleas are in a flock?

Red-billed queleas gather in such huge numbers that it is impossible to count. It can take more than ten minutes for a whole flock to pass by. The red-billed queleas live in Africa, where they can be a huge pest and can destroy large areas of crops. Like all weavers, the male builds a nest by weaving plant material together, and the female inspects it before mating.

Red-billed queleas rest during the day and gather together in flocks at dawn and towards the evening to hunt for food.

▶ How do tree creepers search for food?

Tree creepers spend most of their lives clambering on tree trunks, searching for food in the bark. They have developed a thorough system. They work their way upwards in a spiral, probing crevices with their bills. When it has finished one tree, the tree creeper moves to the next one and starts all over again. Tree creepers' feet have a strong grip and they can hang upside down by their toes, but usually stand upright.

Tree creepers build their nests behind bits of loose bark or in the stems of ivy.

◀ How sociable are social weavers?

Social weavers are arguably the most social birds in the world. They do not just build nests for themselves, but large groups co-operate to build one huge nest for the whole colony, and they sometimes share their nests with other species, who help look out for danger. One nest can be a home for hundreds of individuals and some have remained occupied for more than 100 years. Each nest has its own entrance tunnel, which leads to a separate nesting chamber.

Social weaver birds are master builders. They use large twigs for the nest's roof and dry grasses for the separate chambers.

Courtship displays

Birds display a huge range of behavior when trying to find a mate. Some is quite simple – seagulls just nod their heads, for example. Other behavior is far more complex. Some birds have specialized body parts such as colorful legs or special feathers only used in courting displays. Still others perform elaborate dances or sing songs to win their mates' favors. Many perform combinations of these activities.

▶ Why do cranes dance?

The common crane's mating dance is one of the most complex and is carried out by both sexes. In the mating season, they gather for group displays. Their trumpeting calls can be heard over 1 mile/1.6 kilometers away as males and females each perform a series of graceful, rhythmic leaps, raising their wings in the air and bowing to each other. It looks a little like a crowd of courtiers performing a formal dance. This display demonstrates the cranes' energy and fitness and suitability as mates. Their calls are deep, loud clanging sounds, with trumpeting notes.

Why do frigate birds get puffed up?

Frigate birds have developed a bizarre physical attribute for courtship displays. To attract a female, the male frigate bird perches on a shrub or on the ground and puffs out his large red throat like a balloon. He can stay like this for many hours. If a female likes what she sees, then they mate and build a nest in trees or bushes.

The frigate bird has one of the largest wing-to-body ratios of all birds, making it an expert distance glider.

150

Cranes are tall birds with long legs and a long stride. They are often mistaken for herons, but they have smaller bills and thicker necks.

Where do lyrebirds live?
They live along the eastern seaboard of Australia.

▶ What's superb about a superb lyrebird?

The male superb lyrebird uses a variety of techniques to impress his mate. Much like a bird of paradise, he prepares a display ground with a mound of earth on which he stands and calls for a female. When one appears, he fans his large tail feathers into a bow shape and sings a variety of songs. The lyrebird is a talented mimic and these songs can include copies of many sounds or other birds' songs.

The male lyrebird uses his songs to mark his territory and to warn off rival birds.

151

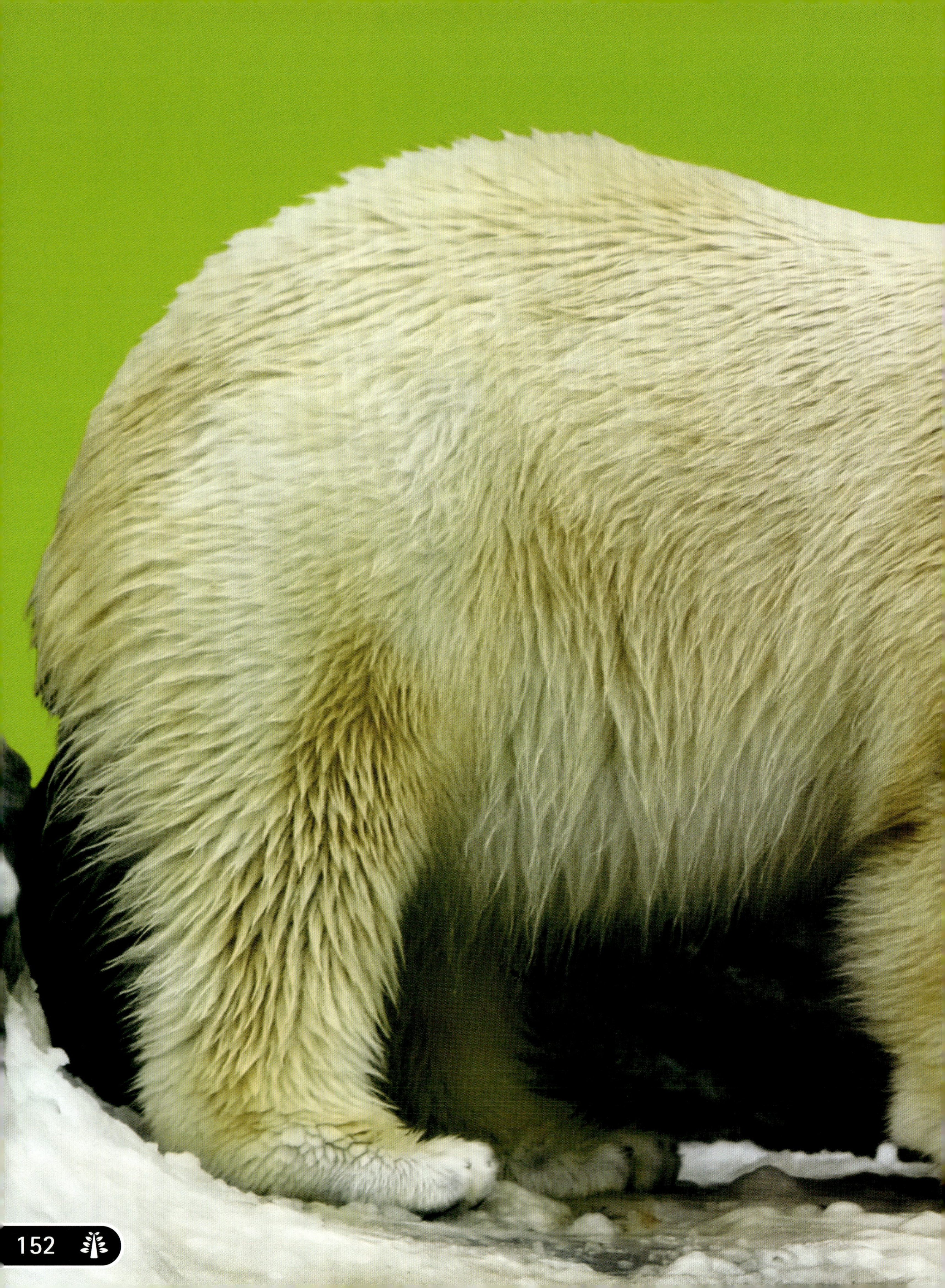

Mammals

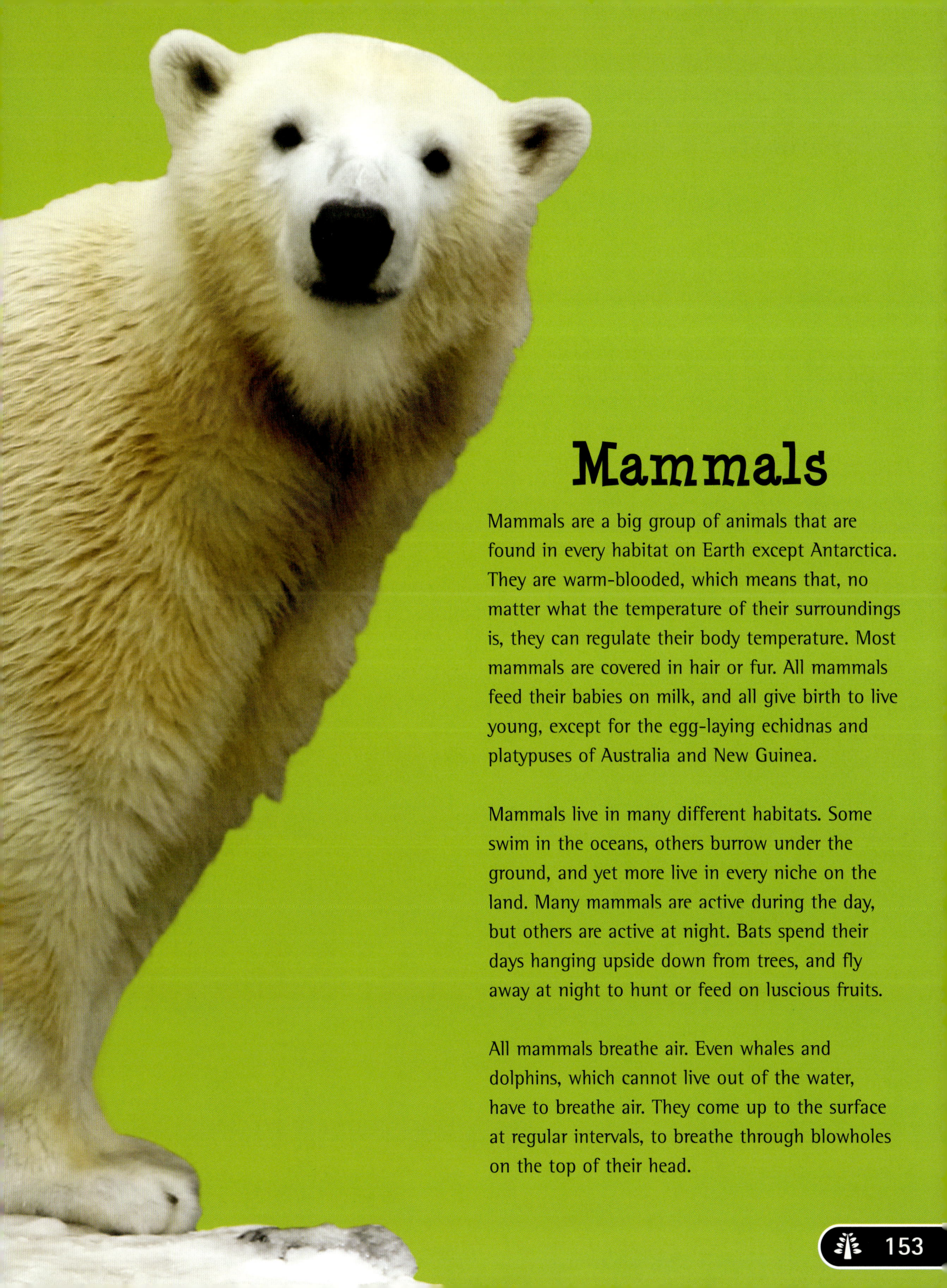

Mammals are a big group of animals that are found in every habitat on Earth except Antarctica. They are warm-blooded, which means that, no matter what the temperature of their surroundings is, they can regulate their body temperature. Most mammals are covered in hair or fur. All mammals feed their babies on milk, and all give birth to live young, except for the egg-laying echidnas and platypuses of Australia and New Guinea.

Mammals live in many different habitats. Some swim in the oceans, others burrow under the ground, and yet more live in every niche on the land. Many mammals are active during the day, but others are active at night. Bats spend their days hanging upside down from trees, and fly away at night to hunt or feed on luscious fruits.

All mammals breathe air. Even whales and dolphins, which cannot live out of the water, have to breathe air. They come up to the surface at regular intervals, to breathe through blowholes on the top of their head.

Platypuses and echidnas

There are about 4,000 different species of mammal, but only three of these species lay eggs to produce their young. These are the duck-billed platypus and the short-beaked echidna from Australia and New Guinea, and the long-beaked echidna from New Guinea. They all belong to a group called the monotremes. It is thought that monotremes have not changed much in millions of years, and could have been around in the age of the dinosaurs.

▼ What does a duck-billed platypus look like?

The duck-billed platypus is a strange-looking creature. It has a flat tail like a beaver, webbed feet and a big beak like a duck, and the furry body of an otter. It lays eggs like a lizard, but feeds its babies milk, like most other mammals.

The female duck-billed platypus doesn't have teats like other mammals, but has a tiny gland on her belly, which oozes milk like sweat. Her beaked babies lap up this milk for about four months, until they can find food by themselves.

▼ Where does a platypus lay her eggs?

A female duck-billed platypus digs a long burrow in the riverbank, with a grass-lined nesting chamber at the end, in which she lays her eggs. As the pregnant female enters the burrow, she blocks it with mud at regular intervals. This keeps water out, warmth in and also protects her eggs and young babies from intruders.

A female platypus lays two or three eggs in her nest. The eggs are very small, not much bigger than marbles. They are soft and leathery to the touch. After about ten days, the eggs hatch. The babies stay in the burrow with their mother for the first four months of their lives.

The duck-billed platypus eats a variety of small freshwater creatures, including shrimp, crayfish, worms, fish and frogs.

Duck-billed platypuses are not sociable animals. Adults do not live in groups, but prefer to live alone in their territories.

154

Where does the short-beaked echidna live?

The short-beaked echidna is more widespread than its long-beaked relative. It lives in most parts of Australia, and also in Tasmania and New Guinea. It is an adaptable mammal, and can survive in many different habitats, such as forests, meadows, deserts and mountains.

The female short-beaked echidna lays a single egg, which she incubates in her pouch for up to 11 days. When the egg hatches, the baby is kept in the pouch for about seven weeks, until its sharp spines begin to grow. The mother then hides her prickly baby in a hollow or cave, returning occasionally to feed it.

Echidnas defend themselves by curling up into a spiny ball, or wedging themselves into a narrow space, so they are hard to get at.

How big is the duck-billed platypus? It grows to about 2 feet/60 centimeters long – about the length of a small dog.

▶ Do long-beaked echidnas have teeth?

The snout, or 'beak', of a long-beaked echidna is about two-thirds the length of its whole head, and it does not have any teeth inside it. Instead, the echidna has a very long tongue, with rows of bumpy spikes on it.

Long-beaked echidnas eat earthworms, and some other small insects. They wrap their tongues around a worm to grip it, then slurp it into their mouth.

Echidnas eat insects, such as ants and termites. Like anteaters, they have long, sticky tongues that help them trap and catch fast-moving prey.

Bandicoots, wombats and quolls

Marsupials are a group of mammals with a pouch on their bellies, which they use to carry around their young. Inside the pouch, the marsupial's baby is safe, and can drink its mother's milk from a teat. Marsupials are a very old order of animals, and one hundred million years ago they lived all over the world. Today, almost all species of marsupial are found in Australia, where there is no threat from larger, more successful mammals.

▼ What do bandicoots look like?

Bandicoots are medium-sized marsupials that live in Australia and New Guinea. They have long back legs, and move by hopping about. A bandicoot's big ears and excellent hearing help it find prey at night, and listen out for predators in the dark.

The long-nosed bandicoot uses its long snout to search for food. It digs holes in the earth with its front paws, and then sniffs out insects and pulls up roots.

▼ What is a quoll?

A quoll is a cat-sized marsupial found in Australia, Tasmania and New Guinea. There are several different species, all with spotted coats. They are all meat-eaters, mainly hunting mice, lizards and snakes.

When a quoll is born, it is no bigger than a grain of rice. There are usually ten babies in a litter, but only the strongest six survive, as the mother only has six teats in her pouch. Baby quolls stay in the pouch for several months.

Long-nosed bandicoots are born after a pregnancy of just 12 days. They grow inside their mother's pouch, drinking her milk for about two months.

Quolls are now endangered, because modern farming techniques are destroying their natural habitat.

A wombat's teeth are like a rodent's – they never stop growing, and are worn down by constant plant-chewing.

▶ Which kind of marsupial lives in America?

Opossums are the only kind of marsupial to live in North and South America – all other marsupials are found in Australia and New Guinea. Some species of opossum have pouches, but others don't. Most opossums live in forests, climbing trees to hunt insects. An opossum will wrap its long, hairless tail around a branch to stop it from falling.

The Virginia opossum has a very interesting defense tactic. When faced with a serious threat, it lies still, pretending to be dead. This puts the predator off, and the Virginia opossum makes a quick escape.

Most species of opossum are about 3 feet/1 meter long, with a very long rat-like tail.

How many species of marsupial are there? There are about 272 species of marsupial in the world, and about 200 of them are found in Australia.

Where do wombats live?

Wombats are ground-dwelling marsupials that live in Australia. They are large, tailless animals, measuring up to 4 feet/1.2 meters long, which is as big as a pig. Wombats are the world's biggest burrowing animals.

The common wombat digs a complex system of tunnels with its strong legs and long claws. It usually lives alone in its big burrow. At night, the common wombat emerges to feed on grasses, roots and fungi.

Kangaroos and koalas

Some of the world's most interesting wildlife is found in Australia, where well over half of all species of marsupial live. Magnificent red kangaroos are some of the fastest animals on land. Their smaller relations, the wallabies, also roam vast areas of Australian grassland. Other memorable and unique Australian marsupials include the sleepy, leaf-munching koala and the fierce, noisy Tasmanian devil.

▼ How far can kangaroos jump?

The red kangaroo is an incredible jumper. A male red kangaroo can cover over 33 feet/10 meters in a single leap – that's almost the width of a swimming pool. Their long tails help them balance as they bound along on their powerful hind legs.

Young kangaroos, called joeys, are only about 3/4 inch/2 centimeters long when they are born. That's about twice the length of your fingernail. When they are born, they crawl into their mother's pouch, and latch onto a teat. Joeys often jump back into their mother's pouch when threatened by predators.

Kangaroos live in the Australian grasslands. They spend their days resting and feed on plants at dusk and during the night, when the temperature is cooler.

Do all kangaroos live on the ground? No, some, like the small tree kangaroos, live high up in the branches of rainforest trees.

The red-necked wallaby was one of the first marsupials to be seen by the European settlers who landed in Sydney Cove, Australia, in 1788.

◄ Are wallabies and kangaroos related?

Wallabies are small members of the kangaroo family. Like kangaroos, wallabies have strong back legs and can leap fast across open grassland. When they want to move slowly, they drop down onto all fours. Both wallabies and kangaroos begin life as tiny, bean-sized babies inside their mother's pouch.

Red-necked wallabies are sometimes called brushers, because they are found in wooded areas and brush rather than rolling, open grassland. They are quite common in the coastal forests of eastern and southeastern Australia.

▶ Is a koala a bear?

No, the koala is actually a marsupial, not a bear. Like other marsupials, koalas carry their small babies in pouches. When a koala baby outgrows its pouch, it hitches a ride on its mother's back as she clambers through the trees.

Koalas are very fussy eaters, and will only eat the leaves and bark of eucalyptus trees. They spend their lives eating and sleeping in the treetops, only coming down to the ground to move along to another clump of trees.

Koalas sleep for about 18 hours a day, and eat whenever they are awake.

How noisy are devils?

Tasmanian devils are famous for the blood-curdling shrieks and growls they make as they gather in groups around a carcass, such as a dead wombat or wallaby. They usually eat at night, searching for food with their keen senses of sight and smell.

Tasmanian devils were once found across Australia but now only live on the island of Tasmania, off the southern coast. They are the top predators there.

Sloths, anteaters and armadillos

Sloths are in the same animal order as anteaters and armadillos. They are grouped together because they all have few or no teeth. Sloths eat leaves and fruit in the South American rainforests. The anteaters of Central and South America survive on a diet of insects, such as ants and termites. Armadillos are omnivorous. Unlike sloths and anteaters, their bodies are covered with tough, bony plates, which protect them from predators.

▼ **How long is a giant anteater's tongue?**

A giant anteater's tongue is an impressive 2 feet/ 60 centimeters long – about ten times longer than your tongue! It is covered with small spines, which point backwards. The anteater's saliva makes these spines sticky, so they are very good at mopping up insects.

Giant anteaters do not live in trees, like their smaller relatives. They live in forests and grasslands of Central and South America, and are active during the day.

▼ **Which species of armadillo is the most common?**

The nine-banded armadillo from North, Central and South America is the most common. In spite of its name, it may have between seven and 11 bands of armor around its body, with an extra 12 to 15 rings around its tail. To escape trouble, the nine-banded armadillo runs faster than a dog.

Nine-banded armadillos dig burrows, in which they rest during the day. They often share their burrow with other armadillos of the same sex, and even with other animals, for example rabbits and skunks.

Giant anteaters walk on their knuckles, so their long claws stay sharp for digging.

Some armadillos roll into a ball when threatened, while others defend themselves with their sharp front claws, or simply bolt for cover in their burrows.

Sloths don't need to excrete their waste very often, which is good, considering how slowly they move! About once a week, they climb down to the ground to relieve themselves. When sloths move on land, they only cover about 6 feet/2 meters per minute. A tortoise can travel at twice that speed.

Where do giant armadillos live?

Giant armadillos live in the Amazon Basin in South America. They can survive in many different habitats, including rainforest and grassland. They are solitary creatures, only coming together to breed.

Giant armadillos are the biggest armadillos. They are almost 3 feet/1 meter long, and weigh about 57lbs/26kg – that is as heavy as a Labrador dog. This large animal's diet is mainly made up of tiny ants and termites, so it needs to eat a lot of them to satisfy its appetite.

The giant armadillo can stand upright on its hind legs and tail to reach up into tall termite mounds. It will also stand like this to warn off predators.

How big are sloths?

Sloths are quite small animals. The southern two-toed sloth is about the size and shape of a small dog. It has a small, round head, a short neck and long limbs. Baby two-toed sloths are just 10 inches/25 centimeters long – about the same size as a rabbit.

Unlike most furry animals, sloths don't groom or clean their fur. Tiny green plants, called algae, grow on a sloth's fur. This provides excellent camouflage as the sloth hangs still in the branches of a tree.

How do sloths hang onto branches? Sloths hook their strong claws over branches so they can hang upside down from them.

Shrews, moles and hedgehogs

Shrews, moles and hedgehogs may look different to each other, but they are actually very close relatives. They are all insectivores, which means their diet is mainly made up of invertebrates, such as earthworms and grubs. These bug-loving creatures are small – hedgehogs grow no bigger than 1 foot/30 centimeters long, moles grow up to 7 inches/18 centimeters long and shrews only reach a length of about 3 inches/7 centimeters. A shrew would sit easily in the palm of your hand, and some would sit on your fingertip!

▼ How many species of mole are there?

There are 26 different species of mole, and they all live underground, in Europe, Asia and North America. They sense vibrations under the ground, helping them find worms and beetles to eat.

Moles have soft, dark fur that was once used to make clothes. It is so short and velvety that it can't be rubbed the wrong way. This means moles can change direction quickly in their underground tunnels.

How are moles adapted to underground life?

Moles are like little, furry digging machines. They have strong bodies, short legs and powerful front paws with sharp claws. Moles have very poor eyesight, but this isn't a problem in the pitch dark. They use their long whiskers to pick up vibrations and have an excellent sense of smell to help them locate prey. Moles dig long tunnels, pushing the loose earth up to the surface to make molehills.

European moles eat at least 50 worms a day. Baby moles are born in a nest, which is called a fortress, which is roughly the size of a soccer ball.

Mole tunnels are very narrow. If a mole needs to turn round, it will do a somersault, or sometimes run backwards!

▶ How much do shrews eat?

Shrews have remarkably big appetites for such tiny animals. Shrews are very active, day and night, and need to eat at least twice their weight in insects every 24 hours.

Shrews have smelly glands on the sides of their bodies, which put off many possible predators, such as weasels, stoats and cats. However, birds of prey and owls don't have a very keen sense of smell, which are a constant danger to shrews as they forage for food.

There are 289 different species of shrew. They are all very small, hungry creatures.

How many spines does a European hedgehog have?
A European hedgehog has about 5,000 sharp, stiff spines all over its back.

▶ How do hedgehogs protect themselves?

When a hedgehog is threatened by a predator, for example a fox, it curls up into a ball. It remains like this until the predator loses interest and goes away. To uncurl, the hedgehog flips over onto its belly, keeping its head and feet tucked in and out of sight. When it is sure the danger is past, the hedgehog scurries off to the nearest hiding place, for example, a bush. Hedgehogs give birth to between four and ten babies, which are born blind and helpless.

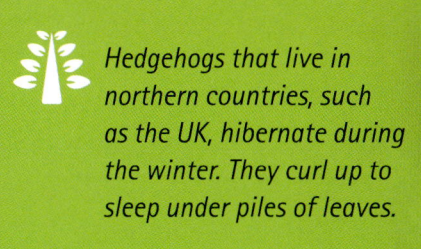

Hedgehogs that live in northern countries, such as the UK, hibernate during the winter. They curl up to sleep under piles of leaves.

Bats and flying mammals

Bats are the only mammals that can fly through the air like birds. Some mammals, such as the sugar glider of Australia and the flying lemur of Southeast Asia, can glide between trees, but do not actually fly. Over one-quarter of all the different species of mammals in the world are bats. Amazingly, there are over 950 bat species.

The pipistrelle bat is common in Europe and eats insects. Its tiny body would fit inside a matchbox!

▼ How do sugar gliders move?

Sugar gliders are small, squirrel-like mammals that live in the forests of Australia and New Guinea. They have a very quick way of moving to the next tree – they simply jump off a branch, and open out their flaps of skin to catch the air, like a parachute. They can then glide down to a lower branch, landing safely on all fours. Sugar gliders are marsupials. The female has a pouch, in which she carries her newborn baby. The baby is tiny at birth, and remains in the pouch for about ten weeks.

▲ Which bat is the smallest?

The world's smallest bat is the hog-nosed bat, sometimes called the 'bumblebee bat'. This rare species lives in Thailand, Southeast Asia. Its wings measure just 6 inches/15 centimeters, and its body is about the size of a walnut.

Most species of bat only have one baby at a time. A baby bat, called a cub, is carried by its mother for the first few weeks of life, but it is soon too heavy for this. It learns to fly at about four weeks old, and begins to hunt on its own.

Sugar gliders nest in groups of up to seven related couples and their babies.

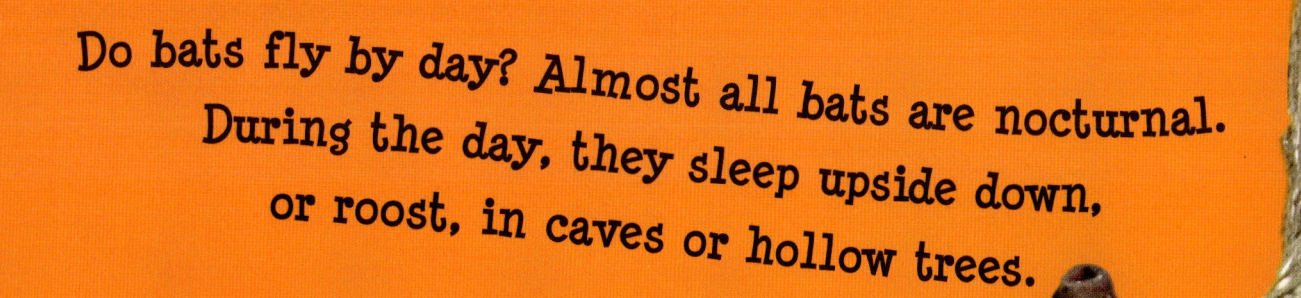

Do bats fly by day? Almost all bats are nocturnal. During the day, they sleep upside down, or roost, in caves or hollow trees.

What are flying lemurs?

Flying lemurs are mammals that can glide between trees. They are not related to the lemurs of Madagascar (see page 223), nor can they really fly. Like bats, they are nocturnal, and roost upside down in the rainforest trees of Southeast Asia. They eat fruit, leaves and flowers. Flying lemurs carry their young until they become independent. A female flying lemur takes her baby with her as she glides between the trees.

☀ *Flying lemurs are also called cologus. The flaps of skin that stretch down each side of their bodies from neck to tail look like a cloak.*

◀ ## How do fruit bats find their food?

Bats have better hearing than most other mammals, but poor eyesight. Many species have unusually large ears, to capture the slightest vibration in the air. Most kinds of bat hunt insects. They make tiny squeaking noises, which bounce back when they touch a flying insect. The bat can then work out exactly where the insect is, and snap it up.

Some fruit-eating bats are known as 'flying foxes'. They have big eyes, long snouts and furry faces, which may have earned them this name. They find their food by smell.

☀ *A bat's wings are made of thin skin, stretched tightly between its legs, tail, arms and fingers.*

165

Rabbits and hares

Rabbits and hares are small, furry mammals with long ears, short tails and powerful back legs for speedy running. Like rodents, they have big front teeth, which never stop growing, and they eat grass, roots and leaves. Rabbits, hares and another little mammal called the pika are all members of the lagomorph order. There are about 79 species in this order of animals.

▼ Where do hares live?

Hares do not dig or live in underground burrows, like rabbits. Instead, they live in open countryside. Hares make a shallow trench in long grass, called a form, where they take shelter and rest. They are well camouflaged sitting in their form, so long as they keep absolutely still.

Baby hares, called leverets, are born above ground, so need to be active and alert from the start. They are born covered in fur, with their eyes open. They can stand and walk just minutes after they are born.

A female hare is called a jill, and a male is called a jack.

Is the black-tailed jackrabbit a true rabbit?

The black-tailed jackrabbit is actually a hare. It lives in many parts of North America, and is considered a pest by farmers, because it will often eat and damage their crops.

During the breeding season, male hares put on fascinating displays to attract the attention of females. They chase each other, leap up in the air, and box each other in fights.

▶ What's a pika's closest relative?

The pika is a small, plant-eating mammal that lives in Asia and North America. It is related to the rabbit, but is much smaller. The large-eared pika is found in the mountainous forests of the Himalayas, in Asia. It is about 8 inches/20 centimeters long, about the same size as a guinea pig.

The pika is a very well-organized little creature. In summer, when it has plenty of food, it sets aside stems of grass, letting them dry in the sun. It then piles the dry grass into miniature haystacks. When winter comes and food is scarce, the pika makes good use of its special food store.

Pikas are also known as mouse hares or conies. North American species often shelter in the gaps between rocks.

How fast can hares run? The North American jackrabbit can reach speeds of 50 miles/80 kilometers per hour – almost the speed limit on USA roads!

The black-tailed jackrabbit's long ears help it control its temperature and cool down in the fierce heat of the North American deserts.

▼ Do rabbits live in groups?

Rabbits are sociable animals, living in family groups of about ten adults and their young kittens. They dig a system of burrows called a warren. There are many separate entrances into the warren, and quick escape routes.

A rabbit prefers to nibble grass and other plants at dusk, or during the night, spending the rest of its time underground in the warren. Rabbits are hunted by many different animals, and are on constant guard against predators.

A female rabbit, called a doe, can give birth seven times a year, and may have up to ten babies in each litter.

Small rodents

Almost half of all the mammal species in the world are rodents. Members of this successful animal family are found in every continent except Antarctica, and live in a variety of habitats, from hot deserts to frozen tundra. All rodents have long, sharp front teeth, which are used for gnawing. Some rodents are small, for example, mice, rats, cavies and lemmings.

▼ How many brown rats are there?

There are more than 50 species of rat, but the two most common ones are the brown and the black rat. Black rats live in warm climates, but brown rats are more adaptable and are found in almost every country. No one knows exactly how many rats there are, but there may be billions – one for every person on Earth.

Wild rats carry about 30 infectious diseases that can be picked up by humans. Rats can also damage crops, perhaps wrecking up to a fifth of all the world's crops every year. It is hardly surprising that wild rats are considered vermin.

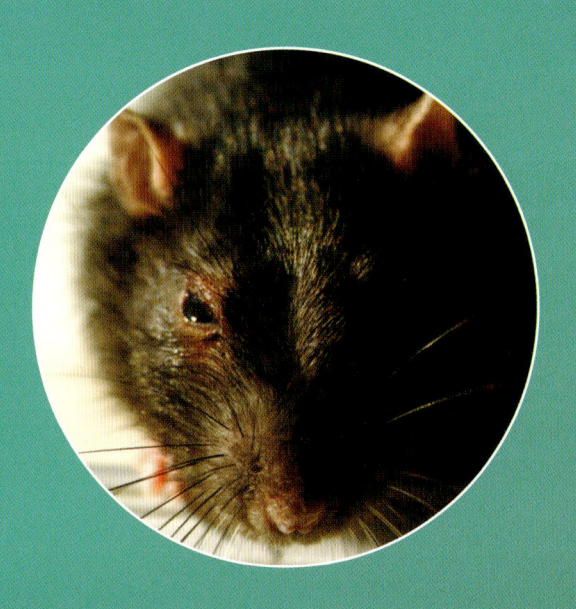

▼ Where do mice live?

There are many different species of mouse, living in a range of habitats, for example, in temperate woodland, tropical rainforest and open grassland. The house mouse is the only species that makes close contact with people. All other species keep well away from human settlements.

Newborn mice are very small and completely defenseless – they are bald, deaf and blind. But in just two weeks, they are bold enough to go exploring. They are ready to have babies of their own at just six weeks old.

Many species of mouse are excellent climbers, such as the harvest mouse. This tiny mouse makes its nest above ground level on grass stems and wheat stalks. It holds on tight with its long, gripping tail.

Black and brown rats have up to 22 babies in a litter, and may have seven litters in a single year. That means every female rat can produce up to 154 babies a year. Fortunately for humans, not all of them survive.

The collared lemming is the only kind of rodent that turns white in winter. This provides good camouflage from predators, such as the Arctic fox and polar bear.

▶ What are lemmings?

Lemmings are a kind of vole, which is a group of over 150 rodent species. Voles have blunter faces, stockier bodies and shorter legs and tails than their mouse relatives. Lemmings live in the far north of America, Europe and Asia. They have very thick fur, and survive the winter cold by burrowing under the snow to find plants to eat.

Large numbers of lemmings live together in burrows, or crevices in rock. When their food supply runs out, usually every three or four years, they migrate in big crowds to find new sources of food. Sometimes lemmings are drowned as they try to cross deep, icy rivers. They do not commit suicide, as some people believe.

Why do rodents have so many babies? Lots of animals eat rodents, so they have large litters to increase their chances of survival.

Many popular household pets are rodents, for example gerbils, hamsters and guinea pigs. Gerbils come from Africa and Asia, hamsters from Europe and Asia, and guinea pigs from South America.

What are cavies?

Wild guinea pigs are called cavies. They are small, tailless rodents that live in the grassland and deserts of South America. Cavies can see, walk and run from the day they are born. This is important, because they are hunted by many predators, such as weasels and birds of prey. Humans also hunt them for their meat. Domestic guinea pigs are now kept as pets all over the world.

Big rodents

Most species of rodent, such as mice, are very small, but some species are bigger. Medium-sized rodents, such as squirrels, chipmunks and prairie dogs, have narrow faces and long, bushy tails. Other large rodents, for example, porcupines and beavers, have blunt snouts and bulky, stocky bodies. No matter how big a rodent is – and some, like the capybara of South America, are as big as sheep – it will still gnaw food with its long, front teeth.

▼ Where do porcupines live?

There are three kinds of porcupine. North American porcupines have short quills and mostly live in trees. Brush tailed porcupines live in Africa and Asia, and can also climb trees. Old World porcupines live in warm areas of Europe, Africa and Asia.

With their 35 inch/90 centimeter long spines, Old World porcupines look like hedgehogs, but they are not related at all. Many will attack if threatened. First, they rattle their quills as a warning, then they run backwards into their enemy to jab it with their sharp spines.

Red and gray squirrels build nests in the treetops, called dreys.

Where do red squirrels live?

Red squirrels live in forests in Europe. They are agile climbers and race up and down tree trunks, clinging on with their sharp claws. Red squirrels are threatened by gray squirrels, which were introduced from North America about 200 years ago. Gray squirrels are much more aggressive than their smaller European relatives. They take over the red squirrels' food supply, forcing them to find new territory. Gray squirrels also pass on a disease which kills many red squirrels.

North American porcupines feed on berries, leaves and bark. Sometimes, they kill a tree by stripping it of all its bark.

◀ **Where do beavers live?**

Beavers are large rodents that live near rivers in northern parts of Europe, Asia and North America. They have very big front teeth, which are strong enough to gnaw through trunks to topple trees. Beavers are specially adapted for swimming, with webbed feet and flat tails.

Beavers are great builders, making homes called lodges from sticks and mud. Beavers build elaborate dams across rivers and build their lodges in the ponds that form behind them. The dams are sometimes over 1,640 feet/500 meters long.

Beaver babies are born in lodges, where they stay hidden until they are big enough to swim out. Young beavers leave their families when they are about two years old.

Do all squirrels live in trees? No, woodchucks, chipmunks, marmots and prairie dogs all live on the ground.

▶ **What is a prairie dog?**

A prairie dog is a burrowing squirrel that lives on the plains and grasslands of North America. It makes yapping sounds like a small dog, which is where this rodent gets its name. Prairie dogs are about 16 inches/40 centimeters long, about the size of a pet cat. They often sit up on their hind legs, to keep a lookout for predators such as coyotes and hawks.

Prairie dogs live in small family groups called coteries. One group's set of tunnels and chambers links up with those belonging to another group, forming a huge network of underground burrows called a 'town'. Prairie dog towns usually have about 1,000 inhabitants. One massive prairie dog town in Texas, USA was thought to have about 400 million prairie dog residents!

If threatened, prairie dogs give an alarm call to warn others in their group. They bounce up and down to make sure their warning is heeded and then run off into their burrow.

Elephants and hyraxes

Elephants are the biggest and heaviest land animals alive today. There are two species of elephant, the African and Asian elephant. Surprisingly, perhaps, the elephant's closest living relative is an animal called the hyrax. This little furry mammal is no bigger than a pet cat, just a fraction of the elephant's size.

It is easy to tell African and Asian elephants apart by the shape of their ears. African elephants have large, rounded ears, and Asian elephants have smaller, triangular ears.

What do hyraxes and elephants have in common?

The hyrax is a small mammal that looks like a rodent, but is actually related to the elephant. Both elephants and hyraxes have tusks, and nails on their padded feet. Millions of years ago, elephants and hyraxes were both enormous. The hyrax got smaller as it adapted to its changing environment, but the elephant didn't!

▲ Where do African elephants live?

African elephants live in all sorts of different environments, from the forests of central Africa to the deserts of Namibia. Different species of African elephant are found in different habitats. The bush elephant lives in grassland, the smaller forest elephant lives in woodland, and the rare desert elephant lives in dry, hot deserts.

The forest elephant is the smallest of all African elephants. This smaller size makes it easier to move between the trees. All kinds of elephant lose heat through their ears, and the bush elephant of the hot savannah needs big ears to lose as much heat as possible. The ears of a forest elephant are smaller, because it lives in a cooler habitat.

There are seven species of hyrax. Some live in rocky mountain areas, others prefer forests. Hyraxes live in family groups, like elephants.

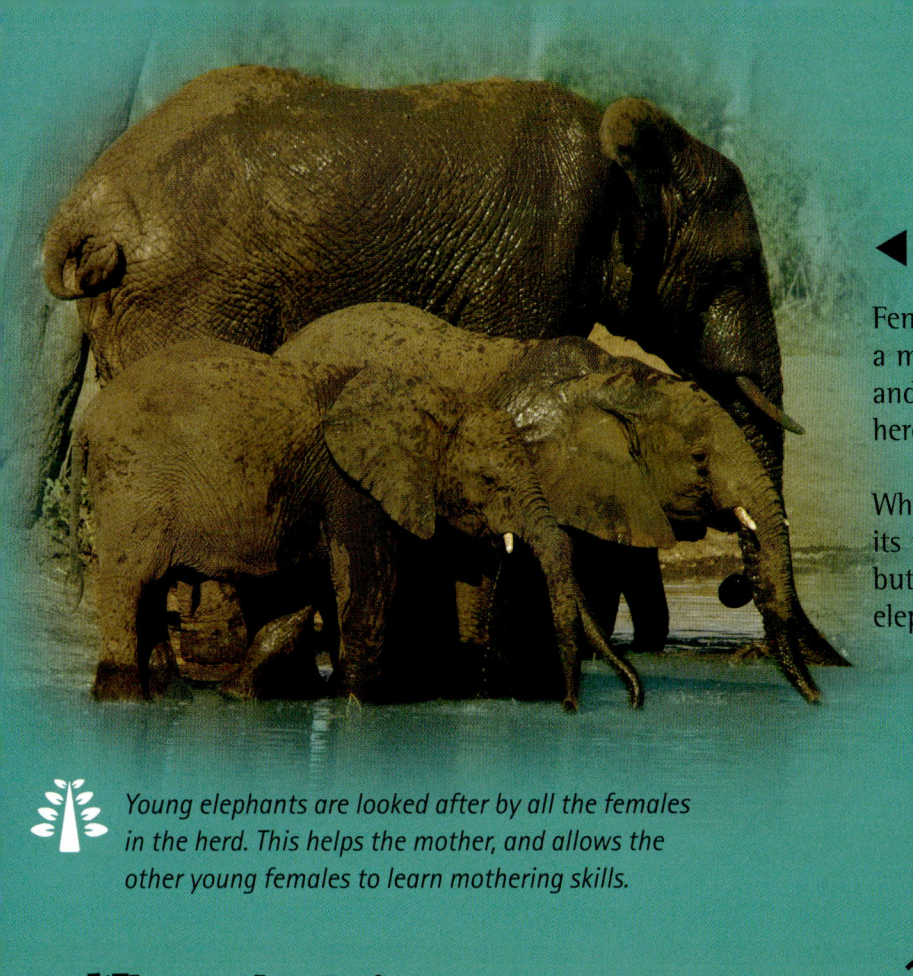

◀ Do elephants live alone?

Female elephants live in herds, led by an old female called a matriarch. The matriarch's herd includes her own young, and her older daughters and their families. Female elephant herds often stay together for many years.

When a male elephant is about ten years old, it leaves its first herd. Young male elephants form their own herds, but they are not loyal to one particular herd. A male elephant may change herds many times in its long life.

Young elephants are looked after by all the females in the herd. This helps the mother, and allows the other young females to learn mothering skills.

▶ Where do Asian elephants live?

Very few Asian elephants are left in the wild. They live in remote, mountainous forests in Southeast Asia (Malaysia, Sri Lanka and Indochina). Like all species of elephant, Asian elephants can travel long distances to find food and water. These journeys, called migrations, happen twice a year, and always follow the same route.

An elephant's long trunk is boneless, and very flexible. It is used for breathing, smelling and drinking. It is both strong and extremely sensitive. It can pull a tough branch off a tree, or pick up a tiny object from the ground.

Asian elephants can be tamed, and have been used for centuries to tow logs and clear forests. In Southeast Asia, they are decorated for festival processions.

How do elephants keep cool? They flap their ears, wallow in mud or splash in water.

173

Horses

Wild horses were first tamed in Asia over 6,000 years ago. Today, there are no truly wild species of horse left in their natural habitat. The Przewalski's horse no longer survives in the wild, and is only found in zoos and wildlife reserves. There are, however, many herds of feral horses roaming free around the world. Feral horses are descendants of tame horses, which escaped from their owners.

▼ What kind of mammal is an ass?

An ass is a wild relative of the horse. There are three kinds of ass – the African ass, the kulan and kiang. Asses live in dry, rocky places, and can survive on very little water. They eat tough, spiky grass to survive in this barren environment.

Asian wild asses are hunted by wolves. They live in large herds and, when they are threatened, a group of strong males gets together to chase away the predators.

▼ Where did the Przewalski's horse live in the wild?

The Przewalski's horse lived in herds on the high grasslands of Mongolia. Today, it is extinct in this habitat, and there are only about 1,600 left in captivity. Attempts are being made to reintroduce this species into the wild.

The Przewalski's horse is smaller and stockier than most domestic and feral horses. But, like all horses, it has very sharp senses. It can see, smell and hear extremely well, and can detect a threat from a great distance.

The Asian wild ass grazes on grass, but will also eat herbs and even the bark of trees when food is scarce.

All members of the horse family have one baby at a time, called a foal. Foals can walk just a few minutes after birth.

How many breeds of domestic horse are there?
There are over 100 different breeds of domestic horse.

Male adult horses are called stallions, and female adults are called mares. Young females are fillies, and young males are colts.

The zebra's black and white coat breaks up its outline, confusing predators by making it hard to spot.

▲ Where do feral horses live?

Feral horses are descended from domestic horses, but they run free in many different habitats, such as dry plains, savannah, wetlands, mountains and even in deserts. All feral horses eat grass, which grows around the world.

Australia has more feral horses than any other continent. The horses are called 'brumbies', and roam throughout Australia's many different habitats. Many herds of feral horses, called mustangs, are also found in the USA.

Is the zebra a kind of horse?

Zebras are members of the horse family. They are smaller than horses, but are a similar shape and have the same kind of feet – soft toes hidden behind hard hooves. Like horses, zebras eat grass.

Zebras are found in Africa, on grassland south of the Sahara. They live in small family groups and, when there is plenty of food and water, several groups will join together to form a herd.

175

Rhinos and tapirs

Rhinoceroses and tapirs are closely related to each other, although they look very different. Both have three toes on each foot, and are quiet, solitary plant-eaters. Both kinds of mammal are quite rare, because they have been over-hunted by humans and their habitat is threatened. Rhinos live in Africa and parts of Southeast Asia, and tapirs live in Central and South America, and also in Southeast Asia.

Rhino horns are made of hair, not bone. These hairs are tightly packed together to make the horn hard and tough.

▲ Are white rhinos white?

White rhinos are gray-brown in color. The 'white' in their name comes from a word in Afrikaans, a South African language. This word means 'wide' and describes the animal's broad lips. White rhinos graze on grass with their wide lips.

Female white rhinos give birth to one calf every two years, and look after it until the next one is born. She can produce up to 44 pints/20 liters of milk a day to feed her baby! Rhino calves may be hunted by lions or hyenas.

◀ Where do black rhinos come from?

Black rhinos are found in central and southern Africa. Their hooked lips and sharp horns make them look fierce, but they eat plants and do not hunt other animals. Black rhinos pull leaves from trees and bushes with their flexible upper lips.

Black rhinos usually live alone, and do not like intruders on their territory. They are fairly short-sighted, and will charge at any moving thing that they don't like or recognize. To make up for their poor sight, black rhinos have good senses of hearing and smell.

Rhinos are different from all other horned animals, because their horns are near their mouths, not on top of their heads. They are famous for their thick skin, which hangs over their bodies like a leathery suit of armor.

Why do tapirs have long snouts?

A tapir's snout is made up of its nose and upper lip. It is very useful for grasping vegetation to bite off and chew. Tapirs eat shoots and leafy plants that grow on the forest floor.

All tapir babies have coats that are covered in a pattern of spots and stripes. This breaks up their outline and makes them hard to see in the rainforest shadows. As the babies grow, this distinctive pattern fades and disappears.

Tapirs are most active at night. They have small eyes, so rely on their sense of smell instead of vision. They keep their noses close to the ground when walking to help guide them.

How big is the white rhino? The white rhino is the second-largest land animal on Earth, after the elephant. It weighs over two tons.

▶ Which tapir is the biggest?

The Malaysian tapir is the biggest species of tapir. It can grow up to 8 feet 4 inches/2.5 meters long, about the size of a donkey. All tapirs have heavy, short-legged bodies, so they can push through undergrowth in the dense rainforests where they live.

Tapirs are good swimmers, and they never stray far from water. They are hunted by big cats, and, if threatened, tapirs plunge into the water and swim – they often get away, because they can swim better than cats.

Tapirs can stay underwater for some time, because they use their long snouts as a kind of snorkel to breathe the air.

Pigs, peccaries and hippos

Wild pigs and peccaries are small, strong mammals with short legs and heavy bodies. The hippopotamus is related to the pig and, despite its large size, it does not eat meat, preferring instead to munch grasses. Pigs, peccaries and hippos are very good at defending themselves. Wild pigs in Southeast Asia can stab tigers with their tusks, peccaries in South America will take on jaguars, and a hippo will fight a crocodile if it has to.

▼ Do hippos like water?

The name hippopotamus means 'river horse'. Hippos spend most of the day in rivers, lakes and ponds across Africa. They keep most of their bodies underwater, to keep cool and avoid getting sunburnt. They leave the water at night to graze on grasses, which they crop with their hard lips.

Hippos are sociable creatures, living in groups of up to 15 animals. Baby hippos weigh about 121lbs/55kg when they are born, and struggle to their feet only minutes after birth. They stay close to their mothers at all times, for protection against predators.

Collared peccaries take their name from the band of white fur around their necks. Their tusks are shorter than those of wild pigs, but still long enough to protect them.

The pygmy hippo's body is narrower and more slender than the common hippo.

How long can hippos stay underwater? The common hippo can stay underwater for as long as ten minutes, without coming up for air.

Where do peccaries live?

Peccaries are medium-sized mammals that look similar to pigs, and even behave like them, but they are not close relatives. They live in Central and South America.

Peccaries live in large herds and will defend themselves as a group, turning together on a predator, such as a big cat. Sometimes a single peccary will charge at an enemy, sacrificing itself to allow the rest of the herd to escape.

▶ Where do wild boars live?

Wild boars live in many countries around the world, usually in forests. They have a coarse coat of brown or gray fur, which hides them well among the trees. Although wild boars have a reputation for being dirty, they will only wallow in mud occasionally, to keep cool.

Female wild boars, called sows, give birth to litters of five or six piglets in grass-lined burrows. Newborn piglets are completely helpless, and stay in their burrow for several days before venturing out. Their coats are stripy, to provide camouflage and give protection from predators.

Wild boars have sharp tusks, which are actually canine teeth that curve upwards out of their mouths.

▼ Why do warthogs have such big tusks?

Warthogs have very long tusks, which are sometimes used to fight off predators. They are also used to dig up food, such as plant roots, in the hard earth. During the mating season, male warthogs use their tusks to fight each other.

Common warthogs live on the plains of Africa, in family groups called sounders. They have three pairs of warts on their faces, and a dark mane that runs down their backs. Their eyesight is poor, but they have a good sense of hearing and smell.

Warthogs sometimes eat their own dung, and the dung of other animals, such as hippos.

Cattle

Cattle are large, plant-eating animals that live in countries all over the world. The first cattle were tamed, or domesticated, by people about 5,000 years ago. Today, wild species of cattle, such as the bison, musk ox and gaur, are becoming increasingly rare. There are about 200 different breeds of domestic cattle, and most are farmed for their milk, meat and hides, although some are still used to pull heavy loads and plough fields.

All species of cattle have four stomachs, to help them digest their food. Grass takes about three or four days to pass through a bison's digestive system.

▲ Are bison endangered?

North American bison were once very common, and lived in herds of up to 100,000 individuals. Unfortunately they were hunted by European settlers to such an extent that only about 1,000 remained. Today, the numbers of bison have increased again, because herds are kept on specially managed farms.

American bison are strange-looking creatures, with huge, stocky shoulders and large heads. Male bison fight for females during the breeding season. They lock heads and push together. The winner is the one that forces the other one backwards. For most of the year, male and female bison live apart in small groups. They spend their time grazing on grasses and plants.

▼ How do musk oxen keep warm?

Musk oxen live on the tundra, the frozen treeless plains of the Arctic. They have thick, shaggy coats of fur which stop them from freezing to death in the sub-zero temperatures.

Musk oxen use their long, downward-curving horns in self-defense. If a herd of musk oxen is attacked by a pack of Arctic wolves, the adults protect their young by standing around them in a circle. They then lower their heads to form a ring of threatening horns.

Musk oxen have extra large hooves to stop them from sinking into the snow.

A herd of gaurs is led by a single dominant bull. A gaur's position in a herd depends on how big it is – the smaller the gaur, the lower its ranking in the group.

▶ Where do water buffalo live?

Water buffalo are found in the wetter parts of Asia and also in Europe, northern Africa, South America and northern Australia. They were once very common in the wild, but now they are mainly kept as working farm animals.

The broad hooves and strong legs of water buffalo make them good at wading though mud and swamps. For many centuries, they have been used to farm flooded rice fields in southern Asia. Like other domestic cattle, water buffalo are also kept for milking.

The water buffalo has the longest horns of any animal alive today – they are about 4 feet /1.2 meters long.

Which is the biggest animal in North America? The bison is. It also weighs more than a small car.

Where do gaurs live?

Gaurs are wild cattle that live in Southeast Asia, from Nepal and India across to Malaysia. They rest at night in forests, moving by day into grassy clearings to feed. These shy, peaceful creatures are hunted by tigers.

Gaurs live in herds of up to 40 animals, and communicate with each other using a number of different sounds, including snorts and growls.

Goats and sheep

Goats and sheep are in a family of animals called bovids – cattle and antelopes are also in this family. All bovids have horns on their heads, which keep growing throughout the animal's life. Goats and sheep have been domesticated for thousands of years. There are many different domestic breeds, but species of wild sheep and goats still live around the world, particularly in mountain areas.

Wild goats, such as the mountain ibex, have hooves that are specially designed for climbing. These hooves have hard edges and soft, rubbery centers, which have a good grip on slippery rocks.

▲ Where do Alpine ibexes live?

Alpine ibexes live in mountain areas of southern Europe, northern Africa and as far east as northern India. During the day, they climb mountain slopes to feed but, by night, they move down to the lower forests to rest. These goats will feed on grasses, leaves, shoots and bark.

In winter, when mountains are covered with a thick blanket of snow, there is no food for the alpine ibex to eat. It moves down to the valleys to graze on the lower pastures.

Female mountain goats give birth to their babies, called kids, on steep cliffs. This helps them to avoid predators. Newborn kids become mobile very quickly, to stay out of danger.

◄ Why are mountain goats white?

Mountain goats have a coat of white wool, which grows especially thick during the winter. The white color provides good camouflage on the snowy mountain slopes of North America, where the mountain goat lives. The main predator of the mountain goat is the mountain lion.

Mountain goats tend to live alone in summer and form large herds in the winter. The sure-footed mountain goat makes its way slowly and carefully through the thick snow, rarely losing its footing on the icy rocks.

▶ Which sheep have spiral horns?

Bighorn sheep live in the Rocky Mountains of North America. Like some other wild sheep, bighorn sheep have long, broad horns, which grow in a spiral at the sides of their head. A ram's horns give away his age, health and how good he is at fighting. Male bighorn sheep fight by charging at each other at speeds of up to 20 miles/32 kilometers per hour. They will do this about five times an hour, sometimes for as long as 24 hours, until one of the fighters becomes exhausted and retreats.

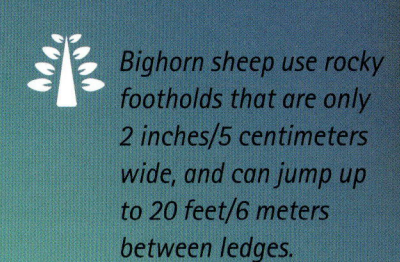

Bighorn sheep use rocky footholds that are only 2 inches/5 centimeters wide, and can jump up to 20 feet/6 meters between ledges.

How many domestic sheep are there in the world today?

There are around 800 million domestic sheep, and over 800 different breeds.

The largest flocks of domestic sheep in the world are in Australia, where there are over 140 million sheep.

Which wild sheep is the smallest?

The mouflon is one of the world's smallest wild sheep. It lives in southwestern Asia and southern Europe. This little sheep was first tamed about 9,000 years ago, and is the ancestor of today's domestic sheep.

Like other wild sheep, the mouflon grows a thick coat of wool every winter, to keep it warm and dry. In the summer, the mouflon sheds its wool to stay cool.

Deer and antelopes

Deer and antelopes are grazing and browsing animals. They are adapted to running, so are good at escaping from danger. Their keen senses help them detect predators at a distance, so they have time to get away. Many species have impressive antlers or long, curved horns on their heads. There are about 36 kinds of deer, and over 100 kinds of antelope.

Male deer are called stags, females are called hinds, and babies are called fawns. They eat leaves and grass for up to 12 hours a day.

Which species of antelope is the biggest?

The eland of central and southern Africa is the biggest species of antelope, measuring up to 6 feet 6 inches/2 meters tall at the shoulder. This large mammal is well adapted to the hot climate, and doesn't need to drink often, because it gets plenty of water from the plants it eats.

▲ How big are red deer?

An adult male red deer has a shoulder height of about 4 feet 4 inches/1.3 meters, and is one of the biggest mammals in Europe. Its big antlers can grow over 3 feet/1 meter in length.

For most of the year, male and female red deer live separately, but they meet together during the mating season. Male red deer fight each other to win a mate. This is called rutting. Older males have larger antlers and win most fights, securing a more dominant position in the herd.

Despite its large size, the eland is surprisingly agile. It can jump over high fences.

If alarmed, a fold of skin on the springbok's back opens to reveal a crest of white hair.

◀ Why do springboks jump?

Like many kinds of antelope, the springbok is very agile, and can jump high into the air to avoid predators. The acrobatic springbok can leap as high as 11 feet 6 inches/3.5 meters – quite a feat for an animal that is only 31 inches/80 centimeters tall.

Springboks live in herds, and are constantly watching for predators, such as lions, stalking them through the long grass. Like other antelopes, male springboks have long, curved horns.

What are antlers made of? Antlers are made of bone and are covered with a velvety skin. Each year, they are shed and a new set grows.

▶ Do moose live in herds?

The moose is the largest kind of deer, measuring up to 6 feet 9 inches/2.1 meters at the shoulder. Unlike other deer, the moose is a solitary animal, living alone except during the breeding season. Moose are found in the forests of North America, and in Europe, where they are known as elks.

A moose's huge, flattened antlers make it look fierce, but the animal is a peaceful plant-eater. In winter, it survives on a diet of roots, bark and leaves, and in the summer it will wade into shallow rivers and lakes to graze on water plants.

The size of a deer's antlers shows how old it is. A bull's antlers indicate its rank within the population.

185

Pronghorns and giraffes

Pronghorns do not have any close mammal relatives and are classified in a family of their own. They are only found in western North America. Giraffes are one of the most unusual animals on Earth. They are so tall that they can see for miles around. These giants of the African savannah tower over their smaller relatives, the okapis, which live in the rainforests of central Africa.

Okapis cannot see very well, but have excellent hearing and sense of smell.

▼ What's special about pronghorns?

The pronghorn is unique – it is the only animal of its type. It looks like an antelope, but it is not a member of this animal family. Pronghorns have distinctive sharp horns that are shaped like meat prongs. Females also have horns, but they are much shorter than the horns of males.

Pronghorns live in deserts and grassland, browsing on vegetation. In the autumn and winter, pronghorns form large herds of up to 1,000 animals.

▲ What's related to a giraffe?

The okapi looks a bit like a horse, but it is actually the giraffe's nearest relative. This shy mammal lives in the rainforest, and does not have the long, thin legs and neck of its savannah cousin. Okapis have the same-shaped heads, and the same short, stubby horns, thin lips and long, grasping tongue as their giraffe cousins.

Okapis are solitary animals that stay in a small area of their natural habitat for all their lives. They keep to well-trodden paths through the forest, as they search for leaves, buds and shoots to eat.

Pronghorns are the fastest mammal in North and South America, reaching speeds of up to 54 miles/86 kilometers per hour.

◀ What's the tallest animal in the world?

The giraffe is the world's tallest animal, measuring a staggering 20 feet/6 meters from head to foot. It has such long front legs that it has to spread them apart to drink at water holes. When it feeds, a giraffe can reach the top of an acacia tree, tearing off the thorny twigs with its tough mouth.

Adult giraffes have only two main enemies – lions and humans – although young giraffes may fall prey to leopards, hyenas or crocodiles. Giraffes aim sharp kicks at predators to defend themselves, or else simply run away from trouble.

The giraffe has a long, grasping tongue, which it uses to pull down the highest leaves from the tallest branches.

Why do giraffes have long tails? Giraffes have long tails to flick away irritating insects.

Giraffes can run at speeds of almost 30 miles/50 kilometers per hour.

For how long are giraffes pregnant?

A female giraffe is pregnant for about 15 months before she gives birth to a single calf. Only an hour or so after its birth, the calf can follow its mother across the grassland.

Giraffes live in small groups of females and their young, led by one male. Males will fight each other to become leader of a group.

Civets and mongooses

Civets and mongooses are small, successful meat-eaters. The two families are not related, but both share similar features – for example, civets and mongooses all have long bodies, short legs, pointed faces and long tails. They are strong, agile hunters with varied diets, and are able to adapt and survive in a number of different habitats.

Yellow mongooses sit up on their haunches to get a better view of their surroundings. They dig long networks of tunnels and chambers underground.

How does the Indian mongoose fight snakes?

When a mongoose confronts a dangerous enemy, such as a cobra, its fur stands up on end, making it appear to be twice its usual size. With a quick darting movement, the mongoose grabs the snake by its neck, biting the back of its head with its razor-sharp teeth. The Indian mongoose has been introduced to many parts of the world to reduce the snake and rodent population.

The Indian mongoose does not just eat snakes. Its diet is also made up of small mammals, insects, eggs and fruit. However, this fierce fighter has been known to attack large animals, such as hares, and even young deer.

The smallest mongoose of all is the dwarf mongoose. It is half the size of its biggest relative. It is only about 8 inches/20 centimeters long.

▶ Do Egyptian mongooses hunt at night?

The Egyptian mongoose is found in most African countries, and also in some parts of southern Europe. It is most active during the night, roaming the land in search of prey. By day, it shelters in burrows, hollow trees and rock crevices.

A female Egyptian mongoose will have a litter of between two and four babies, which are born blind and helpless. The babies do not open their eyes for about eight weeks, but then they develop an excellent sense of sight, which helps them hunt when they leave the nest.

Where do binturongs live?

The binturong is found on many islands in Southeast Asia. It lives in a wide variety of habitats, including forest, brush and grasslands. During the day, the binturong hides in thick undergrowth, but it comes out at night to hunt, sometimes up in the trees. The binturong has a varied diet of small mammals, birds and snakes, as well as insects, eggs and fruit. It usually lives and hunts alone, with males and females only coming together to mate.

Civets can be noisy animals, making four different kinds of sound – a growl, a cough, a scream and a 'ha ha ha' that sounds like a laugh.

Which is the biggest species of mongoose?

The white-tailed mongoose. It is up to 23 inches/58 centimeters long.

▶ Why do meerkats prefer a crowd?

Meerkats are a type of mongoose. Unlike most mongooses, they live in large groups of up to 40 individuals. Meerkats are hunted by larger mammals, such as foxes, so they must always be on the lookout for danger. They are famous for the way they stand up on their hindlegs to keep watch.

Meerkats have long, sharp claws, and often dig for prey on the dry African plains on which they live. Meerkats have a varied diet, and will eat small animals, insects, eggs and plant roots. Like other mongooses, they will attack snakes, but often only to defend themselves from predators.

The name meerkat actually means 'marsh cat', but this animal is not a cat, and it doesn't live in a wet, marshy habitat.

Small cats

Domestic cats are very popular pets, and there are over 500 million pet cats in the world today. Cats that live in the wild are much fiercer than their tame relatives. There are 37 kinds of wild cat, and most of these species are quite small, such as the serval, ocelot, lynx and caracal. Many wild cats have been hunted for their beautiful coats, and now need to be protected in their natural environment.

▼ Why do servals have long legs?

The serval is a small cat with very long legs, so it can pounce on its prey in the grasslands where it lives. This species of cat hunts small rodents and ground-nesting birds, and is able to jump over the tall grass to catch them. Servals have sensitive hearing and locate their prey by sound.

Servals live in the grasslands of central and western Africa. They usually live near water, where leafy bushes grow to hide them from predators. A serval's spotted fur provides camouflage as it sits in the shade.

The serval can leap up to 10 feet /3 meters into the air to catch ground-nesting birds such as francolins.

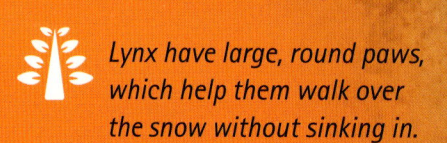

Lynx have large, round paws, which help them walk over the snow without sinking in.

▲ Which cat lives in three continents?

The lynx lives in the mountain ranges of North America, Asia and Europe. A female lynx always gives birth in spring, so her cubs are strong enough to survive the next winter.

Lynxes have unusually short tails, and tufted ears, which make them look different from other cats. In winter, their thick hair grows long, to keep them warm in freezing temperatures. Their fur is a light color, so they are camouflaged in the snowy landscape.

Ocelots can climb, jump and swim well. They usually find a quiet spot in a tree hollow or crevice to sleep during the day.

◀ Where do ocelots live?

The ocelot is a wild cat that lives in the rainforests of Central and South America. Like many other species of cat, the ocelot is threatened by the destruction of its natural habitat.

Ocelots are famous for their beautiful coats. They are reddish brown in color, with black spots and rosettes. They have a single white spot behind each ear and white markings around the eyes and mouth.

Which species of wild cat is the smallest? The rusty-spotted cat is only 14 inches/35 centimeters long, and lives in India.

Cats were first tamed over 3,000 years ago, possibly by the ancient Egyptians.

What do caracals hunt?

This agile cat preys on birds, rodents and small antelopes, stalking a victim before pouncing on it, or knocking low-flying birds out of the air.

Caracals sometimes store the remains of their prey in trees or bushes, so they can return to finish it later. Caracals live in dry scrubland in Africa and southwestern Asia.

Lions, leopards and cheetahs

The cat family includes large, wild cats that are commonly known as 'big cats'. Like their smaller relatives, big cats are meat-eaters, so they must hunt and kill prey to survive. They have keen senses of sight and hearing to help them track down their next meal.

Some big cats, such as the leopard and snow leopard, like to live alone, but others, for example, the lion and cheetah, live in small groups.

How do lions hunt?

Female lions are called lionesses, and they do most of the hunting. They often hunt in pairs, preying on large grassland animals, such as zebra, buffalo and antelope. Lionesses usually hunt at night, and rest during the heat of the day.

A group of lions is known as a pride. In a pride, there are several lionesses with their cubs, and a few males. The males defend the pride, roaring at intruders to warn them away.

Which mammal is the largest predator in Africa? The lion, which has a shoulder height of up to 4 feet/1.2 meters.

Many big cats, such as the lion, are born with spots, which help to hide them from predators. These spots fade with age.

▶ Do leopards live in groups?

No, leopards are solitary animals. They hunt alone, and males only meet with females to reproduce. Leopards live in forests, grasslands and even deserts in Africa and Asia.

Leopards hunt small animals, such as gazelles, pigs and monkeys, but they are not too fussy – they will eat birds or insects if food supplies are scarce. Leopards are great climbers, and will drag their prey up into the branches of a tree to keep it away from hungry scavengers.

The leopard is the most common of all the big cats, and lives in the widest variety of habitats.

The cheetah is the world's fastest land mammal. It can reach speeds of over 60 miles/100 kilometers per hour – but only for about 30 seconds.

▲ Where do cheetahs live?

Cheetahs live in small groups on the vast grassy plains of eastern and southern Africa. They were once common in Asia as well as in Africa, but were hunted so much that they are now a rare species.

Cheetahs hunt by day, because they run after their prey to catch it. They usually hunt small antelope or the young of other grassland animals. When they catch up with their prey, they knock it off balance, then throttle it.

▶ Which is the rarest big cat?

The snow leopard is one of the world's rarest big cats. It lives high up in the mountains of the Himalayas and central Asia. This beautiful animal has been hunted for its thick, winter coat, and is now on the brink of extinction.

The snow leopard's coat gets thicker during the bitterly cold months of winter. The big cat wraps its long, broad tail around its body for extra warmth.

Big cats roar very loudly but, unlike small cats, they can't purr.

Tigers, pumas and jaguars

Tigers, jaguars, pumas and leopards are all big cats. They are meat-eaters, with muscular bodies, and sharp teeth and claws. They creep up on prey, sneaking through the undergrowth, then surprise their victim with a sudden, fierce attack. All these big cats have beautiful markings on their furry coats, which help to hide them in their forest habitat. This makes stealthy hunting a lot easier, and therefore a lot more successful.

The tongue of a big cat is so rough it can rub the meat off a bone.

▲ Are clouded leopards different from other leopards?

Clouded leopards live in forests, not grasslands. They are smaller than other leopards, and have long bushy tails, which help them to climb trees. These tails also make it easier for them to balance up in the branches. Clouded leopards are about 6 feet 6 inches/2 meters long, and half of this length is taken up with the tail. They live in the jungles of Southeast Asia, from Nepal to Borneo.

Which is the largest big cat? The tiger is the biggest. Adult tigers can be about 10 feet/3 meters long from nose to tail.

◀ Where do pumas live?

Pumas live in North America and in most of South America. They prefer to live in wild and remote places, such as wilderness and rocky mountains, where they hunt deer. They are also known as mountain lions, or cougars.

A female puma has a litter of up to six kittens, usually once every two years. The kittens' coats are spotty when they are first born, but become plain after a few months. The mother teaches her young cubs how to hunt, so they can survive away from the family group.

Big cats are very clean animals, and spend lots of time combing their fur with their tongue.

▼ How do jaguars hunt?

Jaguars stalk their prey, attacking with a deadly pounce. But they also use other hunting techniques. Sometimes they lie on branches, waiting to drop down on passing prey. Jaguars have a very powerful bite and can pierce the shells of armored animals such as turtles. They are good swimmers and will chase prey, such as fish, turtles and even crocodiles, in rivers.

Jaguars live all over Central and South America, but their favorite habitat is a thick forest. Like tigers, they are an endangered species, because much of their rainforest home is being destroyed.

Jaguars look like leopards, but are heavier and stockier in build.

What do tigers eat?

Tigers are carnivores, which means that they eat meat. They kill their prey, such as wild pig or deer, by biting into the neck and throat with razor-sharp teeth. Tigers are also very good swimmers, and will hunt in rivers if food is scarce.

Most tigers live in the forests and grasslands of Asia. Their stripy coats hide them in the leafy shadows while they hunt. Siberian tigers live in the taiga of far eastern Russian. All tigers are endangered species.

A tiger can eat a massive 55lbs/25kg of meat in just one meal!

195

Bears

Bears are the biggest meat-eating animals on Earth. There are eight kinds of bear, living in a number of different habitats, including rocky mountains and humid forests. Bears that live in northern parts of the world have thick fur to protect them from the cold. Bears that live in warmer, southern climates do not need to hibernate in winter, as their food supply lasts all year round.

Bears walk with flat feet, so their whole foot touches the ground as they move along.

▼ Can American black bears climb trees?

The American black bear is an excellent climber, using its powerful legs and long claws to grip onto branches and tree trunks. It is also a fast runner, reaching speeds of up to 25 miles/40 kilometers per hour as it chases after prey. However, it mostly feeds on vegetable matter.

Despite its name, the American black bear can be dark- or reddish-brown as well as black. These colors give the big predator excellent camouflage in the mountainous forests of North America, where it lives.

◀ What do sloth bears look like?

Sloth bears have long, shaggy black fur, which camouflages them up in the shady trees. They live in the thick, dry forests of India and Sri Lanka. Unfortunately, they are not as common as they once were.

Sloth bears are agile climbers, and rest in trees during the day. This makes them look a bit like sloths. However, unlike a true sloth, sloth bears are very active when they are awake – they can run faster than humans, if necessary. At night, they spend their waking hours foraging for insects, leaves and fruits on the forest floor.

Most bears have poor eyesight and hearing, but they make up for this with an excellent sense of smell. Sloth bears react aggressively if startled.

▶ Which bear is grizzly?

The brown bear is the most adaptable species of bear, and is found in Europe and southwestern Asia, and across northern Asia to Japan. It also makes its home in mountainous areas of North America, where it is known as the grizzly bear. The brown bear is a skilled hunter, and will eat almost anything.

In its natural environment, the brown bear is at the top of the food chain, and its only enemy is humans. Brown bears have long been hunted for their fur and, for this reason, they are now only found in remote, hilly places.

Grizzly bears like eating fish. Sometimes a grizzly bear will wait by a rushing river to catch a leaping salmon.

How do bears survive the freezing cold winter months? Bears that live in cold places make a den in a cave, then hibernate all winter until the next spring.

Do spectacled bears wear glasses?

No, but they look like they do! The spectacled bear is mainly black, but it has a cream-colored snout and pale rings around its eyes that look like glasses. The spectacled bear hunts at night, and sleeps during the day under tree roots or in rocky caves. The spectacled bear is the only type of bear to live in South America. It is found in several different habitats, ranging from open grassland to humid forest or high mountain slopes.

Spectacled bears live in a warm climate, so they do not hibernate in the winters.

Sun and ice bears

Bears come in a variety of sizes, from the small sun bear, to the towering Kodiak bear. Perhaps the most famous and distinctive bear of all is the majestic polar bear, the huge white predator of the Arctic. This beautiful creature is perfectly adapted to its icy habitat, feeding mainly on seals.

▼ How big are sun bears?

Sun bears are the smallest of the bear family, only 28 inches/70 centimeters tall and up to 5 feet/1.5 meters long from head to tail. They are also one of the rarest kinds of bear, because they have been over-hunted and their Southeast Asian forest habitat is being destroyed.

Sun bears spend their days resting or sunbathing in trees. They are named after the golden crescent patch of pale fur on their chests. They are active at night, searching for insects and fruit and sometimes hunting small rodents, birds and lizards.

Sun bears make cosy nests of leaves and branches in which they sleep during the day. They climb down from their trees to hunt at night.

◀ Which bear is the biggest?

The Kodiak bear is the biggest of all the bears, growing up to 10 feet/3 meters and weighing up to 1,760lbs/800kg. It is a terrifying sight when it rears upright on its back legs, reaching a full height of 13 feet/4 meters. Kodiak bears are found in the snowy mountains of Alaska in North America, and on the islands of Kodiak and Admiralty.

The Kodiak bear of Alaska weighs over three times more than an adult lion.

▶ How do polar bears keep warm?

The whole of a polar bear's body is covered with fur – even the soles of its feet. The hairs are not actually white, but are transparent and hollow, trapping and warming the air inside them. Beneath a polar bear's thick coat is black, heat-absorbing skin and a thick layer of fat.

Polar bear cubs are born in the middle of winter, in dens that their mother has made in the ice. The cubs stay in these dens with their mother, until the warmer spring weather comes. Then they venture out, and begin to learn to hunt.

Polar bears are the only northern bears that do not hibernate during the winter – they are far too busy hunting. During the warm summer months, the food supply drops, so the polar bear rests, living off stores of fat built up during the winter.

Can polar bears swim? Polar bears are excellent swimmers, so they can cross between moving packs of ice in the Arctic Ocean.

Asiatic black bears are in danger of extinction as their habitat is being destroyed by deforestation.

What do black bears do in winter?

Both American and Asiatic black bears hibernate through the winter. Their body temperature and heart rates drop during this special sleep, so they don't use too much energy. They hunt throughout the summer, eating as much food as they can find and catch. The weight they put on during the summer helps them survive their long winter hibernation.

Pandas and raccoons

There are two species of panda. The giant panda is a relative of the bear family. The smaller red panda is more closely related to the raccoon family. Raccoons are very common and familiar animals of North and South America. Most raccoons live in forests, but some have settled in towns and cities, and are considered pests.

The name 'raccoon' comes from a Native American word that means 'scratches with hands'.

▲ What do raccoons eat?

Raccoons are omnivores, and will eat almost anything, for example, fruit, eggs, insects, fish, frogs and clams. They have nimble front paws, with long fingers that can crack open tough shells.

In the wild, raccoons prefer to live in woods, near rivers. They are excellent swimmers and climbers, and are usually more active in the evening. Most male raccoons live alone, only coming together with females to breed. In April or May, female raccoons have litters of four or five babies.

Like other bears, the giant panda has poor eyesight, and uses its sense of smell to find food. Bamboo has little nutritional value, and pandas have to eat a lot to stop themselves starving to death.

Why are giant pandas fussy?

Giant pandas are very fussy eaters, preferring to eat a special type of bamboo that grows in the forests of western China. They need to eat huge amounts of bamboo – every day, they spend at least 16 hours feeding!

Giant pandas are one of the most distinctive animals in the world, with their thick coats of black and white fur. Female giant pandas have one or two cubs at a time, weighing only about 4oz/100g each at birth. The tiny cubs grow quickly, and begin to crawl when they are about ten weeks old.

▶ Where do red pandas live?

Red pandas live in remote mountain forests in the Himalayas, from Nepal to China. Red pandas and giant pandas never meet.

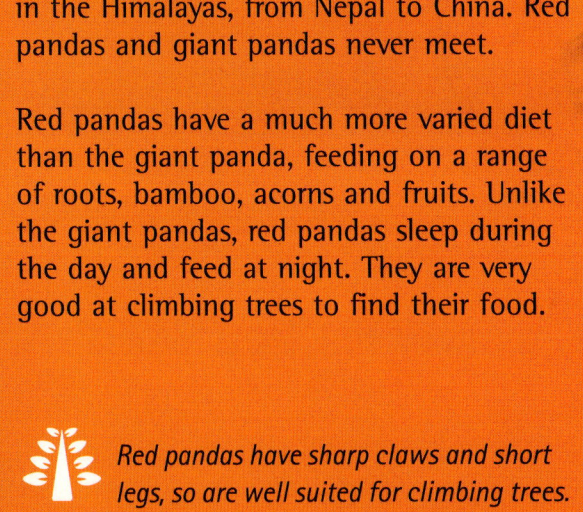

Red pandas have a much more varied diet than the giant panda, feeding on a range of roots, bamboo, acorns and fruits. Unlike the giant pandas, red pandas sleep during the day and feed at night. They are very good at climbing trees to find their food.

Red pandas have sharp claws and short legs, so are well suited for climbing trees.

How many giant pandas are left in the wild?
There are only about 1,000 giant pandas left in the wild.

▼ Do coatimundis eat crabs?

Yes, coatimundis of Central and South America do, but they eat other things too. They can manipulate small prey in their hands, and will sometimes wash food in a river before eating it. Like other raccoons, baby coatimundis are blind and helpless at birth. They feed on their mother's milk for up to four months. Young raccoons leave the nest when they are about eight months old.

Coatimundis belong to the same family as red pandas and raccoons. Although the adults have few predators, their young may be attacked by snakes.

Dogs and foxes

The domestic dog is a very popular pet, and there are over 100 different breeds. But all these pet dogs have just one common ancestor – the wolf. Wolves are one kind of wild dog, and there are 34 other kinds, including foxes, jackals, and dingoes. All wild dogs are carnivores, and are intelligent hunting animals.

Wolves are the largest kind of wild dog. Their sharp fangs and eerie howl sound scary, but wolves rarely attack people.

The desert wolf lives in hot, dry parts of Mexico, Iran and Arabia. It creeps up on its prey as the desert heat means it cannot run for a long chase.

▲ How many wolves in a pack?

Wolves live in family groups. There are usually about 20 wolves in each pack, and at the center is a male and female couple who stay together for life. Their cubs are looked after by all the members of the pack.

Hunting in packs is a very good way of tracking down and killing large prey. Gray wolves will hunt animals that are much bigger than themselves, for example, reindeer and musk oxen. They chase their prey until it is exhausted, then move in for the kill.

▼ Do jackals hunt in packs?

Jackals usually hunt alone or in pairs. They feed on birds, insects, rodents and lizards, but also prey on bigger animals, such as antelope. Sometimes, jackals will get together in larger groups to share the leftovers of a lion's kill.

Jackals are found in Africa, Asia and southeast Europe, where the climate is warm and dry. They live in areas of grassland, where their tawny coat makes them hard to spot. Jackals are often regarded as pests, and people hunt them.

▶ What are dingoes?

Dingoes are wild dogs that live in the Australian outback. They can survive for long periods on very little water, as they get most of the liquid they need from their food. Dingoes have a varied diet, including lizards, birds, rabbits and wallabies. They also attack sheep, and are considered a pest by farmers.

Dingoes are descended from domestic dogs, and may have been introduced to Australia by the aboriginal people 5,000-8,000 years ago.

When were the first dogs tamed?

The first wild dogs were tamed about 12,000 years ago. Pet dogs have played an important part in people's lives for about 5,000 years.

The red fox is found in more countries than any other meat-eating animal.

Where do red foxes live?

The red fox lives in woodland, and is found in many countries all around the world. It is an omnivore that eats small animals, insects and fruit. It is also a scavenger, and has moved into towns and cities, where it forages through garbage cans for food.

Foxes are wild dogs, with excellent hearing, keen vision and a good sense of smell. There are 21 kinds of fox, including the Arctic fox of the far north and the fennec fox of the African and Arabian deserts.

Hyenas and aardwolves

Hyenas are meat-eating mammals. Although they look like dogs, they belong to a completely different family. There are four different kinds of hyena, the spotted, brown and striped hyenas, and the aardwolf. All of these hyenas live in Africa, in dry scrub and grassland south of the Sahara. One species, the striped hyena, is also found in parts of Asia. The aardwolf, although related, has a very different way of life. It lives in eastern and southern Africa and survives on a diet made up entirely of insects.

The jaws of striped, brown and spotted hyenas are so strong, they can crush and eat bones that even a lion cannot bite through.

▲ Where do brown hyenas live?

Brown hyenas live in southern Africa, in a variety of habitats, ranging from woodland and grassland to semi-arid areas. The brown hyena is mostly active at night, when it prowls around, looking for the remains of a kill to scavenge. Its dark coat keeps it well hidden in the dark. Brown hyenas live in small groups, but they do not search for food together. However, if a brown hyena finds a large carcass, it will share it with the rest of its group.

◄ How do spotted hyenas hunt?

Spotted hyenas are social animals, living and hunting in packs of up to 30 animals. They force their prey down to the ground by biting their legs. There then follows a vicious feeding frenzy, with the hyenas tearing the prey to pieces while it is still alive.

Spotted hyenas are sometimes called laughing hyenas because of the cackling noises they make.

Each pack of spotted hyenas has its own fiercely defended territory.

Which is the smallest species of hyena?
The aardwolf is the smallest of the hyena family. It grows to just 32 inches/80 centimeters long.

One aardwolf can eat up to 300,000 termites in a single night.

▼ **What does the striped hyena look like?**

The striped hyena has a paler coat than the brown hyena. It has longer hair, and the shaggy mane on its back can rise up, to make the hyena appear much bigger than it really is. This happens when the striped hyena is threatened.

The striped hyena is not hunted by other animals, but it keeps away from big cats such as lions and tigers. It will chase away predators that are too close to a big carcass, but lets its larger relative, the spotted hyena, eat its food.

With the exception of the aardwolf, all hyenas have sharp teeth that can tear through very tough skin.

What does the aardwolf eat?

The aardwolf is not a scavenger, and doesn't eat scraps from a big cat's kill. Instead, it eats termites, ants and other small insects, which it laps up off the ground with its broad, sticky tongue.

Just like its relative the striped hyena, an aardwolf has a pattern of dark stripes on its pale coat, all over its body and legs. It has a black mane running down its back, and a long, bushy tail. Aardwolves rest by day in underground burrows, often ones abandoned by aardvarks.

Weasels, badgers and skunks

Weasels, badgers and skunks look very different, but in fact they are all members of the same large group of mammals – the weasel family. There are 65 species in this family, including nine kinds of skunk and nine kinds of badger. There are many different weasel-like animals, such as stoats, ferrets, martens and minks. Members of the weasel family are found in every continent except Australasia.

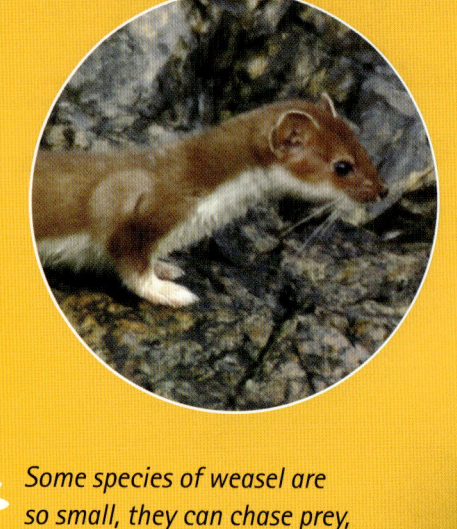

Some species of weasel are so small, they can chase prey, such as mice or voles, down their very narrow tunnels.

Skunks spray their attackers from as far away as 13 feet/4 meters. The strong smell hangs around for days afterwards.

▲ What do weasels eat?

The European common weasel is a fierce hunter, mainly preying on small mammals such as rabbits, rats, mice and voles. They have long, slender bodies and can chase their prey along burrows. They can even make a U-turn in the tunnel if necessary, to make a quick exit. Weasels often hunt by day, and have excellent senses of hearing and sight, as well as smell.

Young weasels live with their mother, sometimes for a while after they have stopped drinking her milk. They learn how to hunt, and small family groups are sometimes spotted hunting together.

◀ Why are skunks so smelly?

Skunks use their strong smell as a form of self-defense. If a skunk is threatened, it will lift up its tail and squirt out two jets of stinking liquid from a hidden gland. The smell is so bad, it forces the predator to retreat.

Skunks live in woods and grassland in North and South America. The most common species of skunk in North America is the striped skunk, but other species include the hog-nosed and spotted skunks. Skunks are small animals, no bigger than a domestic cat.

Where do badgers make their homes?

European badgers live underground in a system of burrows called a sett. They dig the ground with long claws, which they keep sharp by scratching at trees. Badgers are nocturnal animals, eating all kinds of food, but mainly slugs and worms.

Badgers have distinctive black and white stripes running down their faces and necks. In the dark, these stripes look like shadows, camouflaging a badger when it is out at night. Its long body is perfect for moving through tunnels.

A badger's sense of smell is much more powerful than yours – in fact, it is 700 times stronger! Badgers use this super sense to help them hunt in the dark.

What is the smallest carnivore in the world?
The American least weasel – it weighs the same as 10 sugar lumps.

▶ Can minks swim?

The mink is an expert swimmer, with partially webbed feet that are specially adapted for speed in the water. Minks live in burrows that they dig into the banks of rivers and lakes. They hunt a variety of water creatures, including water voles and freshwater fish.

Minks have thick fur, which keeps them warm in cold water. Minks are sometimes hunted in the wild, or bred on farms, for their beautiful fur.

Otters

Otters are members of the weasel family but, unlike other kinds of weasel, they spend more time in water than on land. There are 13 different species of otter. These playful creatures often live in family groups, in large dens near riverbanks. All otters are excellent swimmers, and are able to close their nostrils underwater so they can spend longer foraging for prey. Their long, streamlined bodies are perfectly designed for speedy swimming.

▶ Where do sea otters live?

Sea otters are found in the northern Pacific Ocean, from California to northern Japan. They are strong swimmers, with long hind legs and broad, webbed paws. When they dive for food, they can stay underwater for up to six minutes at a time.

Sea otters eat sea urchins, mollusks and other shelled creatures. They catch their prey with their front paws, then return to the surface to eat it. They crack open the shells on a rock, which they balance on their chests as they float on their backs. Sea otters often keep the same rock tool for many dives.

Sea otters keep warm underwater by trapping a layer of air in their dense fur.

How do European otters hunt?

European otters usually hunt at dusk or during the night, using their sensitive whiskers to feel movements in the water. They are omnivores, eating a diet that consists mainly of fish, but also some river plants, small mammals and insects.

European otters hunt in the water, but they nest on the land. They make covered dens and resting sites in tunnels, tree roots, bushes and rock piles and riverbanks. A river otter has special 'fixed' places for getting in and out of the water, for sunbathing and for sliding on 'otter stairways'.

European river otters make many different types of noise, such as whistles, whimpers, yelps and screams. These sounds are used to communicate with other otters, for example, to greet or warn.

▶ **Why don't clawless otters have claws?**

Unlike other otters, the clawless otter doesn't have claws, and its feet are only partly webbed. It uses its sensitive paws to feel in the mud or under stones on the riverbed, so it can find crabs and other small river creatures to eat. It does not need claws to dig burrows, because it makes its den under rocks or in tangles of vegetation on the riverbank.

Clawless otters have strong, flexible paws that are good for gripping or catching prey.

Which animal has the thickest fur coat in the world?
The sea otter has thicker fur than any other mammal, with about one million hairs per square inch (100,000 hairs per square centimeter).

◀ **How big is a giant otter?**

The giant otter is the biggest species of otter, growing over 7 feet 10 inches/2.4 meters long from nose to tail. It lives in the rivers and lakes of South America. The giant otter prefers to spend nearly all its time in water, and is rarely seen on land.

Giant otters hunt alone in shallow waters but, in deep water, they hunt in family groups. This big animal eats tropical freshwater fish, such as catfish and piranhas, and hunts them during the day. As river and lake water is often murky, giant otters have keen senses of sight, hearing, smell and touch to help them find their prey.

The giant otter lives in a family group of up to eight individuals, with its own home territory. This territory is scent marked, and fiercely protected by the adults.

Baleen whales

Whales are huge mammals that swim in all the world's oceans. There are two main kinds of whale – toothed whales and baleen whales. The biggest, and most famous, species are baleen whales, for example, the blue, gray, humpback and right whales, which take their name from the plates through which they filter their food. Despite their massive size, baleen whales feed on the smallest creatures in the oceans – tiny, shrimp-like krill.

Most baleen whales only have one calf every other year. Calves are born in warm seas, because they don't have much fat, or blubber, to keep them warm.

▼ How do gray whales catch their food?

Gray whales eat similar food to all other baleen whales. Baleen whales feed on krill, which they sift out of the water using huge, comb-like plates.

The gray whale migrates vast distances to find the perfect conditions for breeding. It spends the summer in the Arctic Ocean but, when winter comes, it swims thousands of miles south to the warmer waters of the Pacific Ocean, near California. Here, the female gray whale gives birth to her precious calf. Mother and offspring then swim all the way back to the Arctic Ocean.

The biggest threat to whales is hunting by humans. Many species are now endangered.

▲ How does the right whale breathe?

Like all whales, the right whale must swim up to the surface of the water to breathe. It blows air in and out of its lungs through a hole on its back, called a blowhole. The warm air from the whale mixes with the cold ocean air, forming water droplets. This makes it look like the whale is blowing out water.

Right whales, and all other species of whale, have to rest sometimes. They do this at the surface of the water, with their tails hanging down. This behavior is known as 'logging'.

The humpback whale has the freedom of the sea, and can be found swimming in each of the world's five major oceans.

How do humpback whales attract a mate?

Humpback whales can be very acrobatic, considering their huge size. During the breeding season, they are often seen to leap out of the water. Male and female humpbacks sometimes hold each other tight with their long flippers.

Whales can communicate underwater. The male humpback whale has its own special song, which lasts for about 35 minutes.

Which is the biggest animal in the world?
The blue whale is the largest animal that ever lived.

▶ Are blue whales born underwater?

Like all other species of whale, blue whales are born underwater, coming out tail first so they don't drown in the first moments of life. Blue whale calves grow very quickly, doubling their weight in their first week.

Blue whales are mammals, so their calves drink their mother's milk when they are young. Newborn calves quickly learn to dive down to suckle, swimming up to the surface to breathe afterwards.

Baleen whales are so large, they are not hunted by any other sea creature. A blue whale can live for as long as 80 years.

How big are a sperm whale's teeth?

Sperm whales hunt giant squid. To fight and kill these big underwater creatures, they need to be armed with a set of huge, sharp teeth. A sperm whale has up to 30 deadly teeth lining its lower jaw, each one up to 10 inches/25 centimeters long.

The sperm whale has an enormous forehead, which is not made of solid bone. This part of the head is filled with an oily, waxy substance called spermaceti, which may help to keep the huge creature upright in the water.

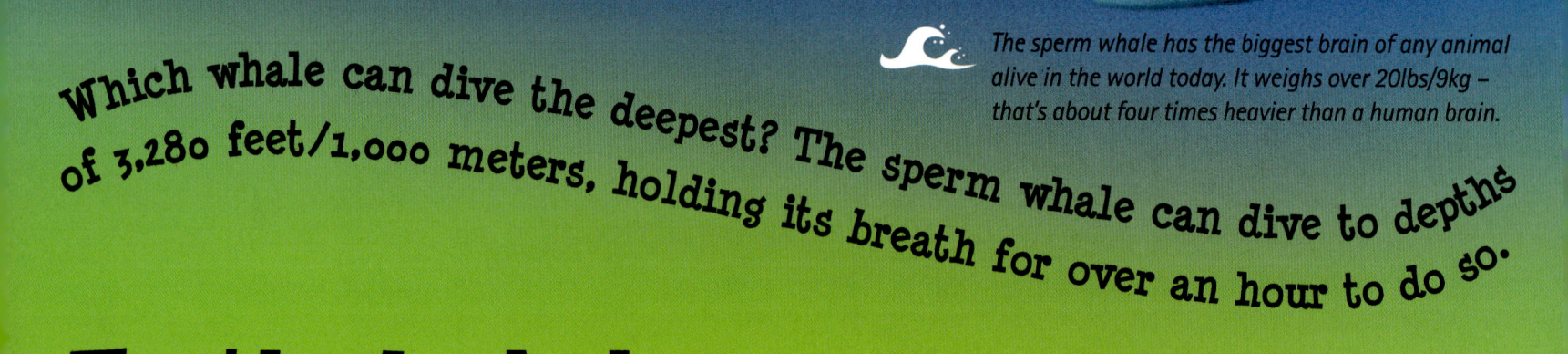

The sperm whale has the biggest brain of any animal alive in the world today. It weighs over 20lbs/9kg – that's about four times heavier than a human brain.

Which whale can dive the deepest? The sperm whale can dive to depths of 3,280 feet/1,000 meters, holding its breath for over an hour to do so.

Toothed whales

Toothed whales, as their name suggests, have teeth in their mouths, and eat fish and other ocean creatures such as squid. Some species of toothed whale dive deep into the water to hunt their prey. Most toothed whales are smaller than their relatives, the baleen whales, although the massive sperm whale is 65 feet/ 20 meters long. That's as long as ten scuba divers lined up in a row!

▼ What do long-finned pilot whales eat?

This species of whale mainly feeds on cod and squid, but also eats other kinds of fish. On average, the pilot whale will swallow about 30lbs/14kg of food in one meal. It will dive over 1,970 feet/600 meters to catch a squid.

Long-finned pilot whales usually live in small groups, called pods, of about six family members. They remain in these pods for their whole lives. However, pilot whales have also been seen to gather in larger groups of up to 50 or more.

The pilot whale gets its name from the time when fishermen followed it to locate shoals of herring in the ocean.

The narwhal's tusk can grow to 10 feet/3 meters long, which is longer than an African elephant's tusk.

▼ Where do beluga whales live?

Beluga whales only swim in the chilly waters of the Arctic Ocean. They stay close to the coast and, in winter, when the sea freezes over, they hunt Arctic fish under thick packs of ice. Beluga whales have a very thick layer of blubber, which protects them from the cold.

The pale beluga whale may look ghostly, but it makes a surprising amount of noise. It has sometimes been called the sea canary, because of the trilling noise it makes.

▲ What does a narwhal look like?

The male narwhal is one of the strangest-looking whales, with a tusk on its snout that is about half the length of its body. It is not clear what this tusk is for, but male narwhals may fight each other with their tusks to win a mate.

Narwhals live in pods of up to 20 individuals. Often, these groups are all-male or all-female but, during the migrating season, many pods may come together to form big crowds of hundreds or even thousands of whales.

Half of a beluga whale's weight is taken up with blubber, a thick layer of fat that covers its body.

Dolphins and porpoises

Dolphins and porpoises are in the cetacean group of mammals. They are toothed whales, with sharp, pointed teeth to help them catch and kill their prey. Most species of dolphin are smaller than their whale relatives, and porpoises are even smaller than dolphins. Porpoises and dolphins have slender, streamlined bodies, which glide quickly through the waves. Fins stand up on their backs to keep them upright in the water.

▼ What do porpoises look like?

The common porpoise looks like a small dolphin, but it has a short snout and a small, cone-shaped head. It usually lives in pairs or small groups, and is not as playful as its fun-loving dolphin relatives.

The common porpoise is not as common as it once was – it is in danger, because it has been hunted so much for its meat and oil. Porpoises also get caught in nets intended for fish, such as tuna.

▼ Are dolphins intelligent?

Dolphins are thought to be some of the most intelligent animals on Earth. A bottle-nosed dolphin's brain is actually larger than a human's.

Like all species of dolphin, the bottle-nosed dolphin lives in family groups, known as schools, sometimes of over 100 individuals. Bottle-nosed dolphins are playful animals, and are often seen leaping out of the water. They swim in shallow waters in both the northern and southern oceans.

Like all whales, dolphins and porpoises breathe through a blowhole on the top of their head. They must come up to the surface of the water to breathe.

Most species of dolphin have about 200 small, sharp teeth in their long, beak-shaped snouts. The teeth are perfectly designed for catching and holding onto prey.

▶ Which dolphins are the best acrobats?

Spinner dolphins are named after the acrobatic, spinning twists that they perform when they leap out of the sea. Spinner dolphins are most active after a rest, and do their most amazing jumps at night. They are sociable animals, and will mix with other ocean species, such as the spotted dolphin.

All dolphins make clicking sounds, which travel through the water and bounce back when they hit nearby objects. This helps the dolphin to track down prey, and to know when there are predators nearby. Dolphins have a sense organ called a 'melon' on their foreheads, which helps them detect the size and position of other sea creatures.

Bottle-nosed dolphins migrate to find warmer waters to breed in. As they do so, they lose weight, so they do not overheat. When they return to cooler waters, they put weight back on, to keep them warm.

Which dolphin is the biggest?
The killer whale is the biggest member of the dolphin family.

Killer whales have very large appetites. A killer whale from the Bering Sea was found with 32 seals in its stomach!

How big is a killer whale?

The killer whale grows up to 33 feet/ 10 meters long, which is about the length of three family cars. It is a fearsome predator and will sometimes hunt in packs to kill animals larger than itself, such as bigger species of whale. The killer whale has a very varied diet, and will eat fish, squid, seals and even birds.

Killer whales live in all the world's oceans, mainly close to the coastline. Sometimes they swim onto the shore to snatch a seal, then let the waves wash them back out again.

Seals, sealions and walruses

Seals, sealions and walruses are all sea mammals, which means that they breathe air, even though they spend most of their time in the water. There are 34 different species of seal, sealion and walrus. They give birth to their young on land, quickly returning to the oceans to hunt for food. Baby seals, sealions and walruses all drink their mother's milk after they are born.

Seals can dive underwater for up to half an hour at a time. Their heartbeat slows down to about 15 beats a minute, so they do not use up much oxygen.

▼ Do elephant seals have trunks?

Elephant seals are named after the males' long, floppy snouts, which look a bit like elephant trunks. Like the elephant, the elephant seal is very big and has thick, wrinkled skin. Male elephant seals are almost twice the size of females.

Living in the frozen waters of the Arctic and Antarctic, elephant seals need a thick layer of blubber under their skin to keep them warm. Elephant seals spend up to 90 percent of their time under water, only coming to the surface to breathe and take short rests.

Elephant seals can make loud sounds through their long, inflatable snouts. During the breeding season, males will challenge each other to a fight with noisy calls.

Why are sealions' flippers like oars?

Sealions use their big front flippers like oars, to propel themselves through the water. A sea lion can swim as fast as 25 miles/40 kilometers per hour. Sealions also use their front flippers to support their bulky bodies as they sit upright on rocks. Unlike seals, they can waddle along on land, again with the help of their flexible front flippers.

◀ **How do gray seals find their food?**

Gray seals have long whiskers, which are so sensitive they detect changes in the water as shoals of tasty fish swim past. This helps gray seals detect and follow their prey. Gray seals eat many different kinds of fish. They bring larger ones to the surface, where they grip them in their front flippers and bite off their heads.

Gray seals give birth to their young on isolated beaches. The young, called pups, are born covered in creamy white fur, which they shed after about three weeks.

Which seal is the heaviest? The elephant seal is the biggest and heaviest seal. The male weighs almost as much as an Asian elephant.

▶ **Why do walruses have tusks?**

The tusks of a walrus are actually long canine teeth. Walruses use their tusks to poke around on the seabed, digging up clams and other shellfish to eat. Walrus tusks are also useful for boring holes in the ice, and for helping a walrus to lift itself out of the water for a rest.

Walruses live in the freezing waters of the Arctic Ocean. They have tough skin, which is about 1 inch/2.5 centimeters thick – and underneath this skin is a layer of fatty blubber to keep them warm.

When walruses lie on rocks to bask in the sun, their skin turns pink. This is because blood is rushing to the surface of their thick skin, to cool their bodies down.

217

Manatees and dugongs

Manatees and dugongs are in the same family of animals, the sirenia. There are only four different species in this family. Manatees and dugongs are more often called sea cows, because these large, gentle creatures spend their time grazing on sea grasses and water plants in shallow, tropical waters. Manatees are found in the warm seas and freshwater rivers of the Americas, the Caribbean and Africa. Their relative, the dugong, swims in the Indian and Pacific Oceans.

What do manatees look like?

Manatees are bulky animals that look a bit like overgrown seals. They grow up to 14 feet 9 inches/ 4.5 meters long, about the length of an Asian elephant. Their flat flippers and tails are rounded, and are used as paddles. Manatees are slow swimmers. They spend all their lives underwater, only surfacing to breathe.

Like whales, manatees and dugongs give birth to their babies underwater. A female manatee will have a single calf, after a pregnancy of about 14 months. A newborn calf suckles its mother's milk from teats just behind her front flippers. It lies beside its mother as it feeds. After three weeks, the baby begins to eat plants, too.

Are sea cows mermaids? In the past, sailors thought sea cows were mermaids, the magical and enchanting female creatures described in old legends.

Manatees have very good hearing. A mother and calf will often squeal to keep in contact with each other when they are apart.

▶ How do dugongs differ from manatees?

The dugong does look similar to the manatee, but there are some differences. Dugongs have a V-shaped tail, and grow two long, tusk-like teeth. They are only found in shallow oceans and, unlike manatees, do not venture into inland waterways.

Dugongs eat sea grasses, usually in water up to 14 feet/5 meters deep. They drift along as they graze, with their flippers hanging downwards.

A newborn dugong will ride on its mother's back down to the seabed, where the mother grazes while the baby feeds on her milk.

▼ Where do African manatees live?

African manatees live along the west coast of Africa, in warm and shallow coastal waters, rivers and swamps. An African manatee spends its life feeding on water plants, eating an incredible eight tons of them a year. This hungry vegetarian lives for about 30 years.

African manatees live in small groups of up to six. When African manatees meet in the water, they touch snouts to greet each other.

Manatees can hold their breath under the water for about 16 minutes before they have to swim up to the surface to snatch a gulp of air.

Manatees shed their skin. This helps to stop the growth of algae on their bodies.

▼ Do Amazonian manatees live in groups?

In the past, Amazonian manatees gathered in large herds but, due to over-hunting, this is never seen today. They are now only spotted in small groups of between four and eight. Humans are not their only predators. Jaguars, sharks and crocodiles also hunt this rare mammal. All manatees are now in danger, and it is illegal to hunt them in many countries.

Camels, llamas and alpacas

The camel family includes the large, desert-dwelling camels of Africa and Asia, and also the smaller, mountain-climbing llamas and alpacas of South America. All members of the camel family are excellent at adapting to very hostile environments. They all have unusually long necks, and their eyes, ears and nostrils are set high up on their heads, so they can spot a threat when it is still a long way off.

The dromedary camel can go for an amazing ten months without water, if it still has access to grazing. When it finds water again, it can drink nine huge buckets in just 15 minutes.

▼ Do Bactrian camels live in the desert?

Wild Bactrian camels live in the Gobi Desert in northern Asia. Conditions in this environment are extreme, with scorching hot summers and harsh, severe winters. The Bactrian camel is well adapted to this varied climate, with long, shaggy fur that protects it from both the heat and the cold.

When strong winds whip up a storm in the desert, it is very important for a Bactrian camel not to breathe in too much sand and dust. To protect itself, it kneels down, presses its ears flat and shuts its eyes and nostrils. Then it simply waits until the storm passes.

▲ How many humps does a dromedary have?

Most camels live in the hot, dry deserts of Arabia and Africa. These camels all have one hump, and are called dromedary camels. They have longer legs, and are not as heavily built as Bactrian camels.

Dromedary camels are useful animals. They are hardy, and can survive high temperatures and harsh conditions. They are famous for carrying heavy loads across the desert, but they also provide their owners with milk and meat. Their hides and hair can be used to make clothes, rugs and tents. Even their droppings can be used as fuel!

Unlike the dromedary, most Bactrian camels are wild, roaming free in their natural desert habitat. Their wide, padded feet stop them from sinking into the soft sand.

▶ Where do llamas live?

Llamas live along the Andes mountain range of South America. These strong animals can breathe the thin air found at very high altitudes. Unlike their camel relatives, llamas do not have humps, but they do have long legs and are fast runners.

Llamas have shaggy fur, which comes in a variety of colors. They are medium-sized animals, about 4 feet/1.2 meters at shoulder height. That is about as tall as a ten-year-old child, but they weigh roughly three times as much.

Llamas were first tamed for human use over 4,000 years ago. They are used to carry goods in inaccessible mountain areas.

What is inside a camel's hump? A camel's hump is a store of fat, not water. When a camel has to go without food or water, it uses this fat reserve to stay alive.

What do alpacas and camels have in common?

Although the alpaca lives in another continent and looks nothing like a camel, the two animals are members of the same family, the camelids. Alpacas and llamas are so alike that they are sometimes thought to be the same species. They are both descended from the guanaco, which was tamed for human use thousands of years ago, but is still found in the wild today.

Like all members of the camel family, alpacas make sounds to communicate with the rest of the herd, such as low, bleating calls to warn of approaching danger.

Monkeys and baboons

Monkeys are sociable animals that live in big family groups. There are two main kinds, Old World and New World monkeys. New World monkeys live in South America, and most have gripping tails that help them swing through the trees. Old World monkeys come from Africa and Asia. Many Old World monkeys also live in the treetops, but some, like the baboon, mostly live on the ground.

▼ Are colobus monkeys good climbers?

The colobus monkey is an excellent climber, and hardly ever leaves the trees of the African forest. Its long tail does not grip onto branches, but it helps the monkey keep its balance high up off the ground, and escape from predators such as eagles and chimpanzees.

Colobus monkeys live in small groups of up to 15 individuals, with one adult male leader, and three or four females with young. The females are close relatives, and will often care for each other's babies soon after they are born.

Colobus monkeys are very noisy, calling loudly at dawn and dusk to mark out their troop territory. They make roaring, snorting, purring, honking and screaming sounds.

◀ Why do mandrills have bright faces?

Mandrills are a species of baboon that lives in the rainforests of West Africa. Male mandrills are twice as big as females, and look very impressive. They have bright red noses and bright blue cheeks, which stand out from their dark fur coats. They also have blue and red bottoms! It seems that all of these markings are there to help a male mandrill attract a much less colorful and interesting mate.

Like most monkeys, mandrills rely heavily on visual or vocal communication to understand each other. Mandrills use a variety of sounds to express themselves.

Why do ring-tailed lemurs have striped tails?

Lemurs communicate with each other using their tails. In tall grass, they point their tails upwards, so the rest of their group can see them.

Baboons spend a lot of time grooming and cleaning each other. This helps them to form bonds in the group, especially between mothers and babies.

▲ How do baboons move?

Baboons live in Africa and the Arabian peninsular. They are large monkeys that live in open country, moving about on all fours. Although they can climb, baboons spend most of their time on the ground, in family groups called troops. Some troops have over 100 members, always led by one male.

Anubis baboons live in troops, protecting them from predators, such as lions. Baboons will also guard their territory, to prevent other baboon troops from straying into it. Baboon troops have a strict hierarchy, and males have to fight each other to earn their ranking in the group.

Are lemurs monkeys?

Lemurs are primates, which is a large group of animals that includes apes and monkeys. However, lemurs are not actually monkeys, even though they look and behave like members of that animal family. Lemurs live in forests on the island of Madagascar, off the coast of Africa. They are not found anywhere else in the world.

Most species of lemur live high up in trees, like monkeys. However, the ring-tailed lemur is different, and spends most of its time on the forest floor.

Lesser primates

Monkeys and apes are in a large group of animals called primates. This group also includes the lorises and tarsiers of Asia, and the potto of Africa. These small, 'lesser' primates are all nocturnal, with large eyes and big ears to help them see and hear in the dark. They live in forests, and spend their time up in the trees. Many lesser primates are now in danger, because their forest habitat is being cut down and they are unable to adapt to any other environment.

◀ How do slow lorises protect their young?

Slow lorises produce a nasty chemical in a gland on their arms. When this toxin is mixed with saliva, it is very unpleasant for predators. Mother lorises lick their babies all over when they leave them, to keep predators away. Animals that hunt the slow loris include sun bears and palm civets.

Slow lorises make very slow, deliberate movements, but when they are close to their prey, such as small birds or mammals, they move swiftly to kill it. Slow lorises have a varied diet, which includes fruit and plants as well as insects and eggs.

Lorises, tarsiers and pottos have opposable thumbs and toes, which can bend round branches to get a firm grip. Their hands and feet are incredibly flexible.

◀ How well can a tarsier see?

Of all the mammals in the world, the tarsier's eyes are the biggest in relation to its body. This nocturnal animal takes in as much light as possible through its large pupils, so it can see well in the dark. This makes it a very successful hunter, good at catching insects, spiders, lizards and small birds.

The Philippine tarsier is found in the rainforests on the Philippines. It is excellent at leaping between branches. Baby tarsiers learn to climb at just two days old, and are jumping after four days. They hunt for themselves at about six weeks old.

The body of a Philippine tarsier is only up to 6 inches/16 centimeters long – about the size of your hand. Its tufted tail is about 10 inches/25 centimeters long.

What does a potto eat?

The potto lives in the tropical rainforests of central and western Africa. It eats mainly fruit, and laps up ants with its tongue. It will also hunt small mammals and lizards. When the potto is looking for food, it moves slowly through the trees. As soon as it spots something tasty, it snatches it quickly in its mouth, or grabs it with both hands.

Newborn pottos cling to their mother's bellies until they are about three weeks old. The mother then leaves her baby hanging on a branch when she goes out to hunt.

Pottos can grip onto branches for a very long time. They have extra blood in their hands and feet, to stop their muscles getting tired.

Why are lesser primates nocturnal?

Small primates are a target for big, strong predators. It is safer for them to hide and sleep during the day.

◀ Where does the slender loris get its name?

The slender loris is so named because it has long, thin arms and legs, which are in fact much stronger than they look. A slender loris can hang onto a branch with one foot as it stretches out to grab an insect, or other tasty snack. Slender lorises live in the forests of India and Sri Lanka. They live alone or with a mate. They spend their days curled up in branches or hollow trees, waking up at night to eat. They are hunted by owls and snakes.

A slender loris's whole body is covered with thick fur, which keeps it warm in the middle of the night, when it is most active.

New World monkeys

New World monkeys live in the forests of Central and South America. All New World monkeys are fantastic climbers, with most species using their strong tails as a third 'arm' to help them grip tightly onto branches. There are many different kinds of New World monkey, including the large spider monkey, the howler monkey and the smaller marmosets and tamarins.

Are monkeys intelligent? Scientists believe monkeys are very intelligent, with large brains for their size, and quick reactions.

▼ How do spider monkeys move?

Spider monkeys have very long arms and legs, and an even longer, stronger tail. They swing through the trees faster than a human can run. They need to move quickly to escape from predators, such as soaring eagles in the skies above, or stealthy jaguars on the forest floor below.

Spider monkeys can also hang by their tails, leaving both hands free to eat food, such as leaves and fruit. When spider monkeys rest, they wind the tip of their tails around a branch, to stop them falling out of the tree.

Black spider monkeys spend almost half of their time resting, and the remainder is evenly split between eating and moving about to find food.

Golden lion tamarins use their long, thin fingers to pick insects out of the bark. They also eat snails, lizards, fruit and leaves.

The howler monkey has a specially adapted voice box, which makes it possible to project sound over a huge distance.

▲ How noisy are howler monkeys?

Howler monkeys make very loud howling noises to warn other troops not to invade their territory. The male leader of a howler monkey troop is the loudest of all. His booming calls can be heard as far as 3 miles/5 kilometers away.

A troop of red howler monkeys usually has about ten members, with only one or two males in the group. Red howlers live high up in the top canopy of the rainforest, where they forage for their favorite leaves, fruit and flowers. They rest a lot, sometimes sleeping for over 15 hours a day.

The pygmy marmoset is the smallest species of monkey in the world. Its body is just 5 inches/13 centimeters long, which is the size of a hamster. This little monkey's tail is about twice the length of its body.

▶ How big are marmosets?

Marmosets are very small monkeys that live in the South American rainforest. They are not much bigger than squirrels. Marmosets have claws on their hands and feet, not flat nails like most monkeys. Unlike other New World monkeys, they cannot grip and swing through the branches with their tails.

Most species of marmoset eat insects, but they will also eat fruit, seeds, sap and gum from bark, if necessary. A mother marmoset will carry her tiny baby on her back while she forages in the trees for food.

Is the golden lion tamarin endangered?

The golden lion tamarin is one of the rarest mammals in the world, with very few left in the wild. They live in the coastal forest of southeast Brazil. Fortunately, golden lion tamarins have been bred successfully in captivity, and can be reintroduced into their natural environment.

Apes

Of all the animals in the world, apes are our closest relatives. apes are intelligent mammals, which can walk upright and live for many years. Apes care for their young in family groups, and are very sociable. Apes are very hairy, and have long, strong arms with shorter, weaker legs. They are great climbers, and live in forests. There are four sorts of ape – chimpanzees, gorillas, orang-utans and gibbons.

Gibbons have long arms which help them swing through the trees.

▲ Which species of gibbon is the biggest?

Gibbons are the smallest kind of ape. The largest species of gibbon is the siamang gibbon, which grows up to 3 feet/90 centimeters tall. That's about as tall as a three-year-old child. Gibbons make up for their small size with speed. They can swing through the trees at speeds of up to 20 miles/32 kilometers per hour. That is a fast sprint at ground level.

There are nine species of gibbon, all of which are known as 'lesser' apes. Gibbons are different from the great apes in that they spend all their time high up in the treetops. They rest sitting upright in the forks of trees.

◀ How big are gorillas?

Gorillas are the biggest kind of ape, growing up to 5 feet 9 inches/1.75 meters tall. That's about adult human height. There are two main species of gorilla, both found in the forests of central Africa. Gorillas live in family groups, led by a single, large male called a silverback.

Baby gorillas are slow developers. They do not walk until they are about ten months old. Young gorillas feed on their mother's milk for about two years, and sleep with their mothers for three years using leafy branches from the forest as bedding.

A troop of gorillas stays in one place until most of the food has been eaten. Then the troop moves on to a new spot, allowing all the plants to grow back.

▶ What do chimpanzees eat?

Chimpanzees live in the forests of central and western Africa, and have a varied diet. Mostly they eat fruit, leaves and seeds, but they also enjoy ants and termites. Sometimes they hunt larger prey, such as bush pigs and small monkeys. Chimpanzees are one of the few mammals to use 'tools' to help them eat. A chimpanzee will use a stick to tease termites out of their nest, and crack open nuts with a stone.

Chimpanzees live in groups of between 15 and 80 family members. Older chimpanzees in a troop can be 60 years old.

Which ape pulls faces? All apes pull faces! The chimpanzee has many different expressions - it can look playful, irritated, angry and frightened.

The name 'orang-utan' comes from the Malay language, and means 'man of the forest'.

Where do orang-utans live?

Orang-utans live in the rainforests of Southeast Asia. But now, as so many of these rainforests have been destroyed, orang-utans are extremely rare. These beautiful, orange-haired primates are well camouflaged in the dark, dappled shadows of their natural habitat.

Like gorillas and chimpanzees, orang-utans make a cosy nest to rest in. Orang-utans search for food at dawn and dusk, but will rest in their nest at midday, and sleep there at night.

Endangered animals

If an animal species is endangered, it means that there are so few of that species left that it is in danger of disappearing forever from our planet. When a species of animal hasn't been seen in the wild for 50 years, it is officially 'extinct'. Every year, more species are added to the endangered list. All animal groups are affected – mammals, birds, reptiles, amphibians, fish and insects. There are several reasons why this is happening, mainly to do with human activity, for example, the pollution or destruction of precious natural habitats.

▼ How many birds are endangered?

One in eight species of birds are endangered, including the largest flying bird of all, the wandering albatross. This incredible bird has a wingspan of 11 feet 6 inches/ 3.5 meters, and glides for thousands of miles across the Southern Ocean. The wandering albatross can live for over 50 years but, sadly, many die much younger than this. Albatrosses often become entangled in fishing lines as they hunt for food.

Wandering albatross chicks take about eight months to become independent. The chicks starve to death if the parents are killed.

The Queen Alexandra's birdwing butterfly is endangered, because its coastal rainforest home is being cleared.

▲ Why must we protect animal habitats?

If habitats are destroyed, so are the animals that live there. The Queen Alexandra's birdwing butterfly is the largest in the world, with a wingspan of 12 inches/30 centimeters. It lives in the rainforests of Papua New Guinea, and only lays its eggs on one kind of vine. It will become extinct if that part of the rainforest, and that vine, is cut down. In the past, this beautiful butterfly was captured and sold to collectors, but this activity is now illegal.

How many endangered species are there? There are over 12,250 endangered animal species in the world today.

There are only about 650 mountain gorillas left in the wild.

▼ How does pollution affect animals?

Pollution in the air, on land and in the sea has a big impact on animals, turning their natural habitat into a dangerous place to live. Many sea turtles, such as the Olive Ridley sea turtle, are killed each year due to marine pollution.

Some species of sea turtle are facing extinction. They are hunted, and many are drowned by accident when they are trapped in fishing nets. Chemical and oil spills poison them, and plastic garbage chokes them.

Why are there so few gorillas left?

There are four species of gorilla, and they all live in the rainforests of central and western Africa. They are threatened by habitat loss, and are also hunted for their meat. Some are also killed or injured in hunters' traps intended for other animals, such as antelopes. The Western and Eastern lowland gorillas are endangered, but the cross-river and mountain gorillas are critically endangered, which means they are close to extinction.

The Olive Ridley turtle population is shrinking fast. It is estimated that there are about 800,000 nesting females left.

231

Conservation

People must act quickly to save many animal species from dying out. Once a species has become extinct, there is nothing anyone can do to bring it back. The situation can seem desperate, with many precious animal habitats disappearing or being damaged by pollution, and some species being hunted to the point of extinction, but there are things that can be done to stop this from happening, before it is too late. The work that people do to help save rare animals is called conservation.

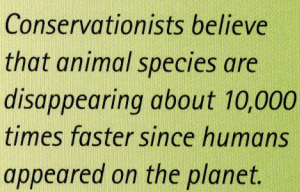

Conservationists believe that animal species are disappearing about 10,000 times faster since humans appeared on the planet.

▲ What is reforestation?

Many governments and environmental groups are planting new trees to replace areas of forest that have been cleared. Reforestation is very important for the future environment, and will save many species from the threat of extinction.

Humans can't be blamed for all extinctions in our planet's history, but we have speeded up the rate of extinctions by the careless ways we treat animals and their environment.

Can we breed rare animals?

Some animals are becoming so rare that they are being bred in captivity. For instance, the Wolong Conservation Centre in southwestern China runs a successful giant panda breeding programme. Pandas are bred and then reintroduced into their natural habitat.

Another example, the European beaver, was almost hunted to extinction, but has now been re-introduced into the wild.

Although it is illegal to hunt endangered animals, the skin, fur, hides or tusks of many rare species are still sold.

232

▶ Why should we save the rainforests?

Not only are the rainforests home to countless animal species, but they add oxygen to our atmosphere, cleaning up the air for all of us. Carbon dioxide from burning rainforests pollutes the air, contributing to climate change.

Many conservation organizations are working hard to save the world's rainforests. You could join one of these organizations to find out how to help.

There is still a lot of rainforest left to save! In South America alone, there is an area of rainforest as big as Western Europe.

How many mammals have become extinct in the last 350 years? About 40 different species of mammal have died out in the last 350 years.

▶ What is a wildlife reserve?

Areas where rare animals live can be protected, and turned into managed wildlife reserves. Hunting in these places is against the law, and the environment is safe from human activity, such as land clearance. In some places, wildlife reserves are big tourist attractions.

Some wildlife reserves are very big. For example, the Masai Mara National Reserve in Kenya, Africa, covers 645 square miles/1,038 square kilometers of savannah and woodland. Endangered animals, such as the African elephant and the black rhino, are protected in this area.

Trade in white rhinos has been strictly controlled and now their numbers are increasing.

Index

A

aardwolf 205
Africa lungfish 80
African elephant 172
African gray tree frog 104
African manatee 219
albatross 131
alligator 122-3
alpaca 221
Alpine ibex 182
Amazonian manatee 219
amebas 14
American black bear 196
amphibians 10, 101-7
angel shark 89
angler fish 87
ant-lion 50
anteater 160
antelopes 184-5
ants 58-9
apes 228-9
aphids 51, 59
Arabian cowrie 25
arapaima 81
Arizona bark (crevice) scorpion 69
armadillo 160-1
armored catfish 95
arthropods 10
Asian elephant 173
ass 174
Atlantic salmon 85
Australian lungfish 81
avacet 133

B

baboons 222-3
Bactrian camel 220
badger 207
baleen whales 210-11
bandicoot 156
barn owl 138
barracuda 98-9
bats 34, 164-5
bears 196-9
beaver 171
bees 56-7
beetles 60-3
big rodents 170-1
bighorn sheep 183
binturong 189
birds 10, 124-51, 230
birds of prey 134-5
bison 180
bivalves 26-7
black bear 196, 199
black rhino 176
black widow 66
black-tailed jackrabbit 166-7
blue whale 211
blue-ringed octopus 28
boa constrictor 113
boars 179
boas 113
bombardier beetle 62
bony fish 10
boomslang 115
bottom dwellers 88-9
breadcrumb sponge 15
breeding 232
broad-headed skink 121
brown hyena 204
brown rat 168

budgerigar 137
bumblebee bat 164
butterflies 54-5

C

caddis fly 50-1
caiman 122
camels 220
canaries 146
cane toad 106
Cape cobra 114, 115
caracals 191
carpet python 112
cartilaginous fish 10
catfish 95
cattle 180-1
cavies 169
centipedes 34-5
chameleon 117
cheetah 193
chimpanzee 229
chipmunk 171
chordates 10
circadas 48
civet 188
classes 9, 11
classification 8-9
clawless otter 209
clouded leopard 194
clownfish 90, 91
cnidarians 10, 16
coatimundis 201
cobras 115
cockatoo 136
cockroaches 44
coelacanth 80
colobus monkey 222
conches 24

cone shells 24
conger eel 94
conservation 232-3
coral 17
coral reef fish 90-1
courtship displays 150-1
cowries 25
crabs 32-3
crane 150
creepers 148-9
crickets 42-3
crocodiles 122-3
curlews 132

D

damselflies 38
Darwin's frogs 105
death's-head hawkmoth 55
deathstalker scorpion 69
deep sea fish 86-7
deer 184-5
dingoes 203
dolphins 214-15
dragonflies 38-9
dromedary 220
duck-billed platypus 154
ducks 130
dugong 218-19
dung beetle 61

E

earthworm 19
earwigs 40
eastern diamond-backed rattlesnake 114
echidnas 155
echinoderms 10
eels 94

Egyptian mongoose 188
eland 184
electric ray 77
elephant seal 216
elephants 172-3
emerald toucanet 142
emperor penguin 127
emperor scorpion 68
emu 127
endangered animals 230-1
European common toad 107

F

families 9
fangtooth 86
feral horses 175
fire salamander 102
fireflies 62
fish 10, 73-99
five-lined skinks 120

flamingos 132
flatworm 10, 18
flies 52-3
flightless birds 126-7
flounder 89
flying fish 97
flying gecko 118
flying lemur 165
flying mammals 164-5
foxes 202-3
freshwater eel 84

freshwater fish 92-3
frigate bird 150
frigate mackerel 83
frogmouth 139
frogs 104-5
fruit bat 165

G

Galapagos tortoise 111
game birds 128-9
gaurs 181
geckos 118-19
geese 130
genera 9
gharial 123
giant anteater 160
giant armadillo 161
giant clam 26
giant grouper 90
giant otter 209
giant panda 200
giant squid 29
giant water bug 49
gibbon 228
gila monster 117
giraffes 186-7
goats 182-3
golden eagle 135
golden lion tamarin 227
golden poison dart frog 104
golden toad 106
gorillas 228, 231
grasshoppers 43
gray partridges 128

great white shark 78
greater Indian hornbill 143
green anaconda 113
green iguana 118
gray seal 217
gray whale 210
grizzly bear 197
grouse 128
guinea pig 169

H

habitats 230
hagfish 74
hammerhead shark 79
hares 166-7
harlequin shrimp 30
hawker dragonfly 38
hawksbill turtle 111
head lice 36
hedgehog 163
helmeted hornbill 143
Hercules beetle 63
hermit crab 32
heron 132
herring 82
hippos 178
hog-nosed bat 164
honeybee 57
hornbill 142-3
horned sun gem 140
horses 174-5
horseshoe crab 71
houseflies 53
howler monkey 227
hummingbird 140-1
humpback whale 211
hunting fish 98-9
hyenas 204-5
hyrax 172

I

iguanas 118-19
Indian cobra 114
Indian mongoose 188
insects 13
invertebrates 13-71

J

jackal 202
jaguar 195
Japanese fire-bellied newt 102
Japanese spider crab 33
jawless fish 10, 74-5
jellyfish 16
jewel cichlids 92
jumping spider 67

K

kangaroos 158
kestrel 135
killer whale 215
kingdoms 9, 10
kiwis 126
koala bear 159
Kodiak bear 198
Komodo dragon 116
krill 30, 31

L

lacewings 50-1
ladybug 60
lamprey 75
lantern fish 84
lantern flies 48
leaf insect 47
leafcutter bee 56
leafcutter ant 58

leafy sea dragon 97
leatherback turtle 110
lemming 169
leopards 193
lesser primates 224-5
limpets 22-3
lion 192
lionfish 91
little spotted kiwi 126
lizards 116
llama 221
lobster 30
locust 42
long-beaked echidna 155
long-finned pilot whale 212
loris 224-5
lungfish 80-1
lynx 190
lyrebird 151

M

magnetic termite 40
Malaysian tapir 177
mallard 130
mammals 10, 152-229
manatees 218-19
mandrill 222
manta ray 76, 77
mantid flies 50
mantids 45
marine iguana 119
marlins 98
marmoset 227
marmot 171
marsupials 157
martin 144
meerkat 189
mermaid's purse 77

mice 168
migrating fish 84-5
millipedes 34-5
mink 207
mole 162
mole cricket 42
mollusks 10
mongoose 188
monkeys 222-3, 226-7
monkfish 89
moose 185
moray eel 94
mosquitoes 53
moths 54-5
mouflon 183
mountain goat 182
musk oxen 180
mussels 27

N

narwhal 213
nemertean worm 10
New World monkeys 226-7
newts 102-3
nightingale 146
nightjar 139
nine-banded armadillo 160
nocturnal birds 138-9

O

ocelot 191
octopuses 28-9
okapi 186
olm 93
opossum 157
orang-utan 229
orders 9
ostrich 126

237

otters 208-9
oven bird 145
owls 138-9
oxpecker 145
oyster drill 22
oysters 27

P

pandas 200-1
parakeet 136
parrots 136-7
pea crab 32
peacock 129
peccaries 178
pelican 131
penguins 127
perching birds 144-5
peregrine falcon 134, 135
phyla 9, 10
pigs 178
pika 167
pike 93
pipefish 96

pipistrelle bat 164
piranha 92
platypus 154
polar bear 199
pollution 231
Pompeii worm 18
porcupines 170
porpoise 214
potto 225
Praewalski's horse 174
prairie dog 171
praying mantis 45
pronghorn 186

puma 194
python 112

Q

quail 129
queen angelfish 91
queen conch 24
quoll 156

R

rabbits 166-7
raccoon 200
rainbow-billed toucan 142
rainforest 233
rats 168
rattail fish 86
rattlesnake 114
rays 76-7
red deer 184
red fox 203
red kite 134
red mysid shrimp 31
red panda 201
red-bellied newt 93
red-billed queleas 148
red-eyed vireo 147
reef squid 28
reforestation 232
reptiles 10, 109-23
rhinos 176
right whale 210
ring-necked parakeet 136
ring-tailed lemur 223
robber flies 52
robin 144
rodents 168-71
roundworm 10

S

sailfish 99
salamander 102
sand dollar 65
scallop 26
scarlet macaw 137
schooling fish 82-3
scorpions 68-9
scorpionfish 91
sea anemone 17
sea cow 218
sea orange 15
sea otter 208
sea slug 21
sea snake 114
sea spider 70
sea star 64
sea trout 85
sea urchin 65
seahorse 96
sealion 216
seals 216-17
serval 190
sharks 78-9
sheep 182-3
shore birds 132-3
short-beaked echidna 155

short-finned Mako shark 78
shrew 162-3
shrimp 30-1
Siamang gibbon 228
Siamese fighting fish 93
silverfish 37
simple animals 10, 14
skate 76-7
skink 120-1
skunk 206
slender loris 225
slipper limpet 23
sloth bear 196
sloths 161
slow loris 224
slow worm 121
slugs 21
small cats 190-1
small rodents 168-9
snails 20
snow leopard 193
social weaver 149
song birds 146-7
species 9
spectacled bear 197
sperm whale 212
spider monkey 226
spiders 66-7

sponge 14-15
spotted hyena 204
springbok 185
springtails 36-7
squid 28-9
squirrels 170
stag beetle 61
stargazer fish 88
stick insects 46-7
sting ray 76
stonefish 88
striped hyena 205
sugar glider 164
sulphur-crested cockatoo 136
sulphur sponge 15
sun bear 198
superb lyrebird 151
Surinam toad 105
swallowtail butterfly 55
swifts 140-1
swordfish 99

T

tapir 177
tarantula 67
tarsier 224
Tasmanian devil 159
tawny owl 138-9

239

termites 40-1
terrapin 110
textile cones 24
thorny devil 116
thrips 36
thrush 144
tigers 194-5
tiger cowrie 25
tiger moth 55
titan beetle 60-1
toad bug 49
toads 106-7
toothed whales 212-13
tortoises 110-11
toucan 142-3
trapdoor spider 66
tree creeper 149
tree python 112
true bugs 48-9
tuataras 120
tuna 83
turtles 110-11

V
veined rapa whelk 23
venomous snakes 114-15
vent worm 19
viperfish 87
vipers 114

W
wall creeper 148
wallaby 158
walrus 217
warbler 147
warthog 179
wasps 56-7
water bear 14
water buffalo 181
waterfowl 130-1
weasel 206
weaver ants 59
weavers 148-9
whale shark 79

whales 210-13
white rhino 176
white-breasted cormorant 130
white-throated needle-tail swift 141
wild dogs 202-3
wildlife reserve 233
willow grouse 128
wolves 202
wombat 157
wood ants 59
woodchuck 171
worms 18-19

Z
zebra 175